A Guide to Self-Improvement in Sermon Delivery

Al Fasol

Baker Book House

Grand Rapids, Michigan 49506

Copyright 1983 by
Baker Book House Company

ISBN: 0-8010-3507-4

Fifth printing, January 1991

Printed in the United States of America

In memory of

R. J. Braasch

Sarah O'Malley

Daisy Rotramel

Alice Hoye

H. C. Brown, Jr.

each a teacher in the profoundest sense of the word.

Contents

Preface

Preaching is a fascinating study that integrates a number of theological and communications disciplines. H. C. Brown, Jr. contended that "True homiletics involves . . . the correct use of Biblical content, hermeneutical principles, theological perspectives, psychological orientation, rhetorical rules, and oratorical principles."[1] This book focuses on oratorical principles; that is, the vocal and physical delivery of a sermon.

Sermon delivery should not be isolated as a homiletic discipline—even for analytical purposes. In fact, the premise of this book is that sermon delivery derives its reason for existence from its relationship to sermon content. That relationship may be specified as one that *maximizes the message and minimizes the messenger.* I admit with chagrin that the opposite is too often true. But that fact simply affirms the need for a

1. H. C. Brown, Jr. *A Quest for Reformation in Preaching* (Waco, Texas: Word Books, 1968), p. 5.

book such as this. The preaching models for too many of us have been, "What I say is not so important as how I say it." To compound this unfortunate approach to preaching, the "how I say it" is usually either: (1) awful, (2) mediocre, or (3) categorized as "the way preachers talk." To further compound the misfortune, many congregations have come to expect that a good sermon is: (1) pious speech that sounds religious, whether or not it is biblical, (2) a performance by the preacher, and (3) a presentation by one who speaks loudly and rapidly in a rough, gravelly voice.

Some people maintain that sermon delivery is a reflection of the preacher's personality and therefore cannot be taught. Not so! Sermon delivery *is* an extension of the preacher's personality, but personalities can and should mature and grow. Improvement in sermon delivery is, of course, one key area in which the person who preaches must grow. Besides, basic speech functions *can* be taught—even to preachers.

As a teacher of homiletics, I admit that I cannot teach basic motivation for preaching. Much of the success of preaching depends on the individual's inner drives. A study of sermon delivery can be helpful in improving the techniques of communication. In fact, sermon delivery that is forceful, appealing, and clear is a blessing to any congregation. But excellence in delivery should spring forth from the minister's dedication to his divine call to preach. The success of preaching lies in one's inner sense of dedication, not in the mastering of speech techniques. This book merely seeks to enhance the dedicated, divinely called preacher's ability to communicate. We have already established the definite need for that enhancement.

I have intentionally often used the word *speaker* synonymously with the word *preacher* because this book is written for anyone in God's service who wishes to improve his/her ability to communicate. *Speaker* is used when application can be made beyond preaching. *Preacher* is used when application should be made primarily to the preacher.

One goal of this book can be stated both positively and negatively. I hoped to produce a book that will immediately help the preacher improve sermon delivery. I hoped not to produce another boring speech book. I look forward to responses to the book from future students, for they assuredly will relate to me how close my ambitions for this book have come to being achieved.

My appreciation is extended to a colleague, Dr. Jimmie L. Nelson, for his critical reading and pertinent suggestions. Appreciation is also due to Mrs. Mary Anne Barroz, who typed the syllabus that grew into this book, and who typed the early drafts of this manuscript. Gratitude is also expressed to Mrs. Dedra Pease and Mrs. Barbara Walker for typing the final manuscript. As always, responsibility for the final product is mine.

The sermon itself is the main thing: its matter, its aim, and the spirit in which it is brought before the people, the sacred anointing upon the preacher, and the divine power applying the truth to the hearer—these are infinitely more important than any details of manner. Posture and action are comparatively small and inconsiderable matters; but still even the sandal in the statue of Minerva should be correctly carved, and in the service of God even the smallest things should be regarded with holy care.

Spurgeon
Lectures to My Students

1 A Theology of Delivery
"Why should I study sermon delivery?"

Sermon delivery is the servant of sermon content. This relationship must be understood and practiced if preaching is to be effective. *What* we preach is always more important than *how* we preach. Note carefully that the relationship between content and delivery is stated in the comparative degree. Content is *more* important than delivery. Delivery *is* important, but content is *more* important. This basic and specialized statement of a theology of proclamation is the premise of the book. The purpose of this chapter is to present a basic theology of preaching. As with any theology, a theology of preaching has several avenues of approach. In this chapter we will discuss why we preach, what we should preach, who should preach, and the way we preach. Our working definition of preaching is: *Preaching is a word from God applied to a contemporary congregation, communicated by a God-called person in a way that maximizes the message and minimizes the messenger.*

Why We Should Preach

God ordained preaching as a means of revealing Himself to mankind. At least some of the unrecorded questions of the church at Corinth dealt with preaching in general and its content in particular. Paul answered many of those questions in I Corinthians 1:21b: ". . . it pleased God by the foolishness of preaching to save them that believe." Paul's play on words (exegete this verse to understand what Paul meant by "the foolishness of preaching") tends to detract us from the questions the Corinthians obviously and justifiably had raised: "Why did God choose vicarious death on a cross as a means of redeeming the world? Why would He have us hear of the atoning death through the voice of other persons called preachers?" The simple answer is: ". . . it pleased God." The final answer, of course, is much more complex. Of necessity, it will be left to the reader to do further study.

The efficacy of both the content and the purpose of preaching has been questioned by every generation of Christians since the time of the Corinthians. Yet preaching remains a characteristic of Christianity. This persistence of preaching can be traced to its origins which lie in Hebrew oral traditions and in Hebrew prophecy. These were spoken in a tenacious spirit and on the authority of: "Thus saith the Lord. . . ."

God's initiative is evident in even the oldest records of man speaking for Him. Moses, for example, wondered who would hear him when he spoke for the Lord: "Please, Lord, I have never been eloquent, neither recently nor in time past, nor since Thou hast spoken to Thy servant; for I am slow of speech and slow of tongue" (Exod. 4:10, NASB). God's answer was: "Now then go, and I, even I, will be with your mouth, and teach you what you are to say" (Exod. 4:12, NASB). Later, God declared: "I will raise up a prophet from among their countrymen . . . and I will put My words in his mouth, and he shall speak to them all that I command him" (Deut. 18:18, NASB). Centuries later, the credentials of Amos as a prophet were questioned by Amaziah. Amos answered that his authority for speaking for God came from God Himself: "But the LORD took me from following the flock and the LORD said to me, 'Go prophesy to My people Israel'" (Amos 7:15, NASB).

The roots of Christian preaching may lie in Hebrew history, but the form of Christian preaching is indelibly influenced by Greek rhetoric. Oration existed prior to the Greeks, but it was Korax in 466 B.C. and Demosthenes and Aristotle in the fourth century B.C. who crystallized the rules of rhetoric that have had a vast influence on speech making and preaching to this day. Preaching historian E. C. Dargan observed:

> It [oratory] was cultivated in all the Greek countries, but reached its highest stage of development at Athens, and its personal acme in Demosthenes. Along with the practice of public speaking came the theory, the reduction to principles and rules, the teaching of rhetoric as an art. It is a notable coincidence that Demosthenes, the greatest orator of ancient times, and Aristotle, the great philosopher, and author of the most original and suggestive treatise on rhetoric in ancient literature, should have lived at the same time and died the same year, 322, B.C.. With the passing away of these masters, and the political overthrow of ancient Greece, the oratory of the Greeks rapidly degenerated. But its lasting impress had been left on the history of oratory, and of civilization.[1]

The Greek influence on Christian preaching came gradually, and it was certainly felt by the end of the second century. It may be detected for instance, in the preaching of Origen. When Origen announced a biblical text, made some preliminary remarks, delved into the "higher" meanings of the text, and concluded with a challenge, he was using many of the rules of rhetoric formulated by Koras in 466 B.C. Many sermons to this day bear Grecian influence: introduction (preliminary remarks), body (usually three rhetorical divisions),

---

1. Edwin Charles Dargan, *A History of Preaching From the Apostolic Fathers to the Great Reformers A.D. 70–1572* (New York: A. C. Armstrong & Son, 1906), pp. 16-17.

conclusion (often a poem for beauty and appeal, or a 'sob' story for pathos, or both), and an invitation to act on that which has just been preached.

Since apostolic times, preaching had to withstand both friends and foes of the pulpit. Foes of the pulpit have delivered predictable indictments such as these: the monologue approach is obsolete, preaching is irrelevant, and preaching needs more visual and less auditory stimuli. Where these and other criticisms have been accurate, preachers have benefited. When the criticisms were not accurate, preaching was harmed little by it.

It is interesting that the monologue approach to preaching has survived as well as it has. True, some classroom teachers use a strictly monologue approach, but many of them encourage conversation, dialogue, or question-and-answer sessions. The classroom is not exclusively manned by a bald-faced professor with lecture notes. The classroom is often a place where ideas are exchanged between teacher and student as well as between student and teacher. The church sanctuary, on the other hand, is rarely used for dialogue. Dialogue, a response in the form of questions or comments from the congregation, was not uncommon in Old Testament or New Testament times. Even later, "St. Augustine was known to ask questions of the people present. . . ."[2] With the possible exception of a brief period in medieval times,[3] dialogue preaching is relatively new. "Formal pulpit dialogue, essentially a recent development, may be an outgrowth of the historic Christian concern for the unchurched, and a chance to come to grips with their thinking."[4] The monologue approach survives because true Christian preaching is empowered by the Holy Spirit and based on the living Word. Preaching is relevant because Scripture is

2. Richard Leliaert, "The Dialogue Homily: Theory," *Preaching,* Vol. 2, No. 1 (January-February, 1967), p. 20.

3. See George Hedley, *Christian Worship* (New York: The MacMillan Company, 1953), p. 190; and George W. Barret and J. V. Langmead Casserly, *Dialogue on Destiny,* (New York: Seabury Press, 1955), pp. 10-11.

4. William D. Thompson and Gordon C. Bennett, *Dialogue Preaching* (Valley Forge, Pa.: Judson Press, 1969), p. 19.

relevant. Even so, the argument for more visual and less auditory stimuli may have some validity. Visual aids are not uncommon in the pulpit, but they are hardly prevalent either. The use of visual stimuli calls for careful architectural planning so that everyone in the congregation can see. However, visual aids are helpful when used effectively.

Occasionally, the friends of the pulpit have inadvertently caused preachers to reassess themselves and their task as much as their foes have. This was often caused by an emphasis on a particular style of preaching. Origen, for instance, soared into the stratosphere of allegory. He felt that Scripture had three levels of meaning: the literal or obvious meaning; the moral meaning, which applies the text to the congregation; and the spiritual or higher meaning, which was discovered by the allegoric method. Chrysostom and Augustine explored the inner sanctum of the individual psyche. A thousand years of monasticism darkened the world with Bibleless pulpits, Luther brought in vulgarity along with the vernacular to his polemical approach, and Calvin brought an architectural system of institutionalism which existed until Whitefield took preaching into the open fields of Britain and America. American preachers strived valiantly to have preaching become the standard of culture in the eighteenth and nineteenth centuries.

Preaching has also survived a number of attempts to disassociate it from theology. "Whether seen as Christianized rhetoric (as in the influential nineteenth century homiletician, John Broadus), a plain conduit for the *real* Word of God (as in many Barthian and a few Lutheran theologians), or as an exercise in speech and communication (as in many seminary curricula), preaching suffers a certain theological homelessness. . . . Since its relationship to theology is seldom mentioned, much less seriously analyzed, preaching endures its *de facto* exclusion quietly, without argument."[5]

Preaching and theology are as vital to one another as

5. Richard Lischer, *A Theology of Preaching* (Nashville: Abingdon Press, 1981), pp. 13-14.

inhaling is to exhaling. All of the theological disciplines are focused in preaching. The preacher must remember that a majority of the congregation is confronted by theology only in the form of a sermon. Therefore, the preacher must be well read in all phases of theology—Bible, ethics, history, so that the sermon is as rich and effective as it ought to be.

What We Should Preach:
A Word from God
Applied to a Contemporary Congregation

Where does a preacher find a word from God? The answer is: from the Bible. Space is not available for us to discuss the various presuppositions preachers bring to the Bible. Nor is there enough room to discuss the veracity of extra-biblical sources of eternal truth. For most of us, the Bible is at least the primary (if not the only) source for the text of a sermon. We will therefore discuss what a biblical text is and how it relates to a sermon.

The word *text* is derived from the Latin word, *texere,* meaning "to weave." The text is woven into the sermon. The length of the text is usually determined by its immediate context. One criterion for selecting a text is to determine whether or not it is a complete unit of thought. That would protect the preacher from isolating and distorting the meaning of a text. For example, ". . . there was a silence in heaven . . ." is too brief to be a sermon text. An adequate text would have to deal with the cause for that silence. This fragment of Revelation 8:1, however, could be the focal passage in a text.

Occasionally, the text may be too lengthy for one sermon. The preacher may opt, in these situations, to preach from focal passages within the text. A sermon on the revival on Mount Carmel, for instance, might have a text that is three chapters long. The preacher could summarize large portions of text and then read the focal passages to be developed in the sermon. When determining the length of the text, be certain that the text is a complete unit of thought—whether it be a verse, a sentence, a paragraph, or longer passage.

The relationship between the text and the sermon developed from it is crucial but may have varying degrees of strength. A sermon that communicates the essential ideas of the text may be said to have a *direct* relationship to that text.[6] The sermon and the text say the same thing. For instance, a sermon titled, "The Christian Attitude Toward Service," might be based on Mark 10:35-45. Verses 42-45 could be the focal passages. The objective of the text, and therefore the sermon, would be for the hearer to adopt a lifestyle reflecting Jesus' teaching that true greatness comes through humble service. The *direct* biblical sermon develops the key idea or central thrust of the text.

It is possible to preach a biblical sermon that has less than a direct relationship to the text. Luke's primary purpose in recording Acts 11:22-27 may have been to preserve the historical events that led to our being called Christians. A focal passage could be 11:24a "For he [Barnabas] was a good man, and full of the Holy Ghost and of faith. . . ." The sermon would explore the meaning of "good," why Barnabas was so designated, and what kind of person would be considered "good" today. This approach develops an *implication* or *suggestion* of the text rather than its direct thrust.

These are just two options available to the preacher in the preparation of sermons. Many creative ways can be used to prepare and preach biblical sermons. The preacher should carefully study all of these options. They are superior to the common practices of lazy or ignorant preachers who lead congregations to form false concepts of preaching.

The pulpit orator should avoid a number of faulty methods of presenting a text. One shoddy model is the practice of announcing a text, reading it, and then abandoning it. Another

6. For a full discussion of the relationship between sermon and text, see chapters 5 and 6 of *A Quest for Reformation in Preaching* by H. C. Brown, Jr. (Nashville: Broadman Press, 1968).

is reading a text and then attaching subjective ideas to it, no matter how remote their connections to it might be. In this instance the preacher generally says, "Here's what I see. . . ." The personal authority of the preacher is not nearly so strong as, "The Bible says. . . ."

I once heard a sermon on the commandment "Thou shalt not steal" in which the outline was:

1. Thou shalt not take anything without permission.
2. Thou shalt not borrow anything and not return it.
3. Thou shalt not play Bingo lest thou take something from someone who is trying to take something from you.
4. Thou shalt not collect trading stamps and redeem them for merchandise that you do not pay for.

Predictably, the last two points were prefaced with the remark: "I get something different from the text. . . ."

Granted, biblical interpretation is always subjective. But there are varying degrees of subjectivity. A sound exegetical approach that includes careful linguistic, lexical, historical, and theological study will minimize subjectivity. Scripture is not ". . . of one's own [*idios*] interpretation" (II Peter 1:20b, NASB).

Allegorizing or typologizing a text should also be avoided. Allegory is defined as the figurative treatment of one subject under the guise of another. Matthew 8:24-26 is one passage that is often allegorized. The stormy sea in this allegory becomes the world; the ship is the church being tossed about by the waves of the world. The danger of allegory is that it invites the interpreter to make the Bible say anything the reader wants it to say.

Typology is related to allegory, but does not pose quite so serious a problem for hermeneutics. Typology expects Scripture to contain some symbolic significance or representation. The strength of typology is found in the way it opens the door to a creative and fresh approach to a text. But the accuracy of the text should never be sacrificed for creativity. For example, many preachers use a typological approach to Genesis 22:1-18. Isaac is described as a "type" of Christ because Isaac was an only son about to be put to death. That is a valid similarity. This text however, emphasizes the obedience, faith, and reaffirmation of God's covenant with Abraham. The usual typological approach to this passage raises these questions: (1) Has the text been developed accurately? (2) If Isaac is a type of Christ, then how is Abraham, who is about to slay the type of Christ, to be described? As a type of sin? As a type of Satan? (3) What is the purpose in making Isaac a type of Christ in this text when so many other passages about the Savior could be selected?

The chief danger of typology is the impression it lends that one can make almost anything out of any text one desires to make. Much can be preached from Genesis 22 and any other biblical text without the imposition of typology. A major danger of using typology is that it overemphasizes secondary ideas in the text. Allegory and typology, if used at all, should be limited to illustrating the sermon rather than shaping the entire address.

The degree of importance we attribute to the relationship between text and sermon is intrinsically involved with what we think preaching should be and accomplish. Many preachers find pleasure in sloganeering ("I just want to preach the simple gospel," or "I just want to preach God's Holy Word"), but very few do exactly that. We all can spout clichés about preaching, and we would profit from examining what we mean by those clichés. And in so doing, we must be careful not to spawn more clichés.

What should preaching be, and what should preaching do? The answers are varied. We might say, "Preaching should be Christ-centered." "Preaching should confront people with the Word of God." But what does "Christ-centered" mean? Quoting Scriptures about Christ? Sharing testimonies about Christ? Teaching about Christ? And what does "confront people" mean? Should we offer the Word of God on a take-it-or-leave-it basis? Should we attempt to persuade people to accept Christ? If so, when does persuasion become coercion or exploitation?

Answering the question, "What should preaching be and what should preaching do?" is difficult but extremely worthwhile. We can profit from the pilgrimage of others here.

Domenico Grasso concluded: ". . . the object and content of the preaching of Jesus and the Apostles is the person of Christ."[7] "Unlike all other messages, the Christian message is identified with the Messenger, with the person of Christ."[8] According to Grasso, preaching should be identifiable with Christ.

Karl Barth felt that preaching should be the speaking of the Word of God. This speaking should involve the listener in the Word of God in a way that removes the barriers of time. In true biblical preaching, Barth contended, the listener should not think in terms of first century and twentieth century, but consider the central truth of the Word of God. Barth felt that biblical preaching dissolves the wall between the first-century word and twentieth-century man.[9] But what should preaching do? "What is transmitted and what one seeks to have accepted is a person. And the goal to be obtained is adherence to a person . . . the real problem of preaching consists in discovering how to . . . establish between God and man a community of life, so that man will not think of or see himself except in the light of God. . . ."[10]

Schleiermacher felt that preaching should be an opportunity for the Word to rise forth from the spiritual union of the preacher with his listeners, and that preaching should give expression to the life in which preacher and congregation are thus joined.[11]

7. Domenico Grasso, *The Preaching of God's Message* (South Bend, Indiana: University of Notre Dame Press, 1965), p. 8.

8. Ibid., p. 20.

9. Cf. particularly *The Preaching of the Gospel*, trans. B. E. Hooke (Philadelphia: The Westminster Press, 1963); *The Word of God and the Word of Men,* trans. Douglas Horton, 1938; and *Church Dogmatics,* vol. I, pt. 1, trans. G. T. Thomason (New York: Charles Scribner & Sons, 1936).

10. Barth, *The Preaching of the Gospel,* p. 21.

11. For example, see *Religion: Speeches to its Cultural Despisers,* translated by John Omen (New York: Harper, 1958); George Cross, *The Theology of Schleiermacher*

Does Schleiermacher sound a little "heady," and more than a little idealistic? Clyde Fant agrees: "The passionate desire to insure that the pure word of God is proclaimed to the congregation has resulted in an almost superstitious depersonalization of the act of preaching. As a matter of practical fact, the Word does not 'arise out of the Bible and proceed into the congregation.' It proceeds into the congregation on the words of a very subjective human being who has struggled to interpret those words which he has found in the Bible and which God graces with his presence as the Word."[12]

These excerpts are included to stimulate the preacher's thinking about what one preaches. Such evaluation will sharpen understanding of the relation between text and sermon. Nebulous thinking will lead to nebulous preaching, and nebulous preaching is never appropriate. The content (what we preach) of our sermon needs to be strong, clear, and text-centered.

Who Should Preach: A God-Called Person

Phillips Brooks has given us an excellent broad definition of preaching. He defined it as ". . . the communication of truth by man to men. It has in it two essential elements, truth and personality. Neither of those can it spare and still be preaching."[13] We have already discussed Brooks' concept of "truth," what should be preached. We will focus now on the words *communication* and *personality* from his definition.

Communication is a diverse discipline that is foundational to preaching. When we preach, all that we are as a Christian person is focused on communicating a message from God. Our childhood experiences, our conversion experience, our models in preaching and pastoring, our self-image, our perception of

---

(Chicago: The University of Chicago Press, 1911); and Schleiermacher's *Liturgies: Theorie & Praxis* (Gottingen, Vandenhoeck, and Ruprecht, 1963).

12. Clyde Fant, *Preaching for Today* (New York: Harper and Row, 1975), p. 33.

13. Phillips Brooks, *Lectures on Preaching* (1914; repr. ed., Grand Rapids: Baker, 1978), p. 5.

what preaching should be and what preaching should do, and our various academic and theological disciplines are just a few of the resources we call on as we prepare to preach. Then as we present the sermon these resources are brought into tension with individuals who have their own varying perceptions of who they are, who and what the preacher is, what preaching should be, and what it should do. Our varying backgrounds will either assist the preacher in achieving desired responses from the congregation or, at times, hinder the preacher from achieving desired responses. They may even elicit an undesired response from the congregation.

Communication is a fascinating, complex process. Broadly defined, *communication* means "to pass along information by talking, writing, or gesturing." The process is not automatic. The following illustration touches one important aspect of the communication process.

Shortly after becoming a Christian, a young man felt a desire to share his new knowledge of God with someone other than regular church attenders. An idea gradually developed. He would hold Sunday school at 5:00 on Sunday mornings for boys aged 9-15 who sold Sunday newspapers. He knew that he would have to cultivate their confidence, so he made it a habit to stop by the newspaper office and purchase a paper on his way to his own job. He also had to work on Sunday, for he signed a local radio station on the air at 7:00 A.M. Eventually, he suggested to the boys that they have Sunday school when they arrived for work at 5:00. They usually spent the first thirty minutes idly waiting for their newspapers to arrive anyway. The idea received little enthusiasm but no resistance. Rather than have them study from formal literature, he decided to discuss basic biblical concepts with them. The first lesson was to be about God, so he decided to tell them that God is like a father. His own experience had led him to this analogy. Of course, he did not think his father was God. He appreciated his father's love and vision for his future, so he thought the analogy was appropriate. But when he opened the first lesson by saying God is like a father, he immediately lost credibility with those boys because their experiences with their fathers were not at all like his. Their fathers forced them to work early on Sunday mornings and then, by Sunday afternoon, they usually took the money they earned.

An important communication process was involved in speaking to those boys. This process is called "encoding-decoding." Encoding, the initial step in this process, occurs when the speaker seeks to determine which words will best convey a message. The listener's process of interpreting those words is called decoding. Ideally, the encoding is done so effectively that the decoding leads to a complete understanding of the message intended by the encoder. The young man in the preceding illustration made the mistake of adhering to only the first part of this dual process. He should at least have said, "God is like a good friend." The boys' decoding of "friend" would have been much better than their decoding of "father."

Preaching in a way that communicates is a dual process that continues during the sermon itself. We invest all that we are in sermon preparation, but as we do we must be sensitive to the needs of the congregation.

I do not know how to define "God's call" to preach, nor can I articulate my own call to anyone else. Research on the subject seems to verify that no one else knows how to describe God's call either. The frustration of trying to explain to someone a call to preach is analogous to a child asking a parent, "How do you know when you are in love?" The answer, "You will know when it happens to you" may be plausible, but it will be unsatisfactory to the person asking the question. For my own call, I had no beam of light from heaven as did Joan of Arc. Nor did I hear a voice, as did Saul of Tarsus. I do know this: I did not one day simply reflect on my future vocation and of my own volition decide that preaching is what I wanted to do in my life. For me, while I was praying one Sunday night I knew that God wanted me to preach. I cannot tell anyone how I knew, but I knew.

I also know that I would not presume to preach if it were not for this experience of God's call. Some persons do choose on their own to be preachers, but I cannot understand their presumption—much less how they are able to survive without the sustenance of a divine call. Preaching is one of the most demanding, frustrating, gratifying, and fulfilling jobs in the world. No one should presume to be a preacher without being specifically led in that direction by God. Beyond the call to preach, several other personal dynamics are involved in determining *who should preach*.

Effective preaching integrates the pastoral role with the preaching role. The person who preaches must be in contact with the congregation at other times than the preaching hour. The more effectively we minister with people—whether in times of great tragedy or great joy—the more effective we will be as preachers. Some preachers say, "My gift is preaching. I don't excel as pastor." Others say, "I am not good at preaching, but I do minister to the people." No one is free to be a good preacher but a poor pastor; nor is one free to be a poor preacher but a good pastor. Effective Christian preaching combines careful preparation with a sensitivity to the needs of our listeners and a sensitivity to our own needs. These are extremely complex issues for which we can derive working (but not final) answers. The working answer is this: continue your own spiritual growth, keep in contact with your congregation at all levels (counseling, teaching, and fellowship), and maintain study habits in various theological disciplines that will enrich your sermon preparation. The communication process is a constant challenge. Our success as God-called communicators of God's word will be directly affected by the amount of investment in study and pastoral care that we put into our calling.

How We Should Preach:
Maximizing the Message
and Minimizing the Messenger

Sermon delivery derives its importance from its relationship to sermon content. *The goal of sermon delivery is to maximize the message and minimize the messenger.* The messenger is a critically important part of the preaching process, but the messenger is never more important than the message. As sermon delivery derives its importance from its relationship to sermon content, so the messenger derives importance from the message to be delivered. The preacher, for instance, is not like a mail deliverer. The person who delivers mail has a noble vocation, but once the mail is delivered the task is completed. The preacher's responsibilities continue beyond the mere delivery of the message. The preacher may be compared to an ambassador who represents higher officials, nations, or kingdoms. The ambassador is entrusted to speak for another. The ambassador cultivates relationships with those being represented and also with those who receive this representative. These relationships assist the ambassador. First, they help the ambassador know who is being represented and why. When the ambassador conveys a message, it is more likely to be communicated accurately and efficiently. Second, those who receive the message need to know something about the messenger. The ambassador therefore must convince those receiving the message that the messenger is a person of expertise and integrity, and possesses deep convictions about the message being delivered.

But what are the criteria for measuring effectiveness in delivery? Are these criteria always subjective? Will they be the same in all preaching situations? in all denominations? in all regions of the country or world? for all of the various styles of preaching? The complexities are endless, but some guidelines are available. They will be discussed in the next chapters of this book.

One additional aspect of sermon delivery should be discussed here. Much of the communication of a sermon takes place before the first word is preached. The pastoral role produces varying relationships between pastor and congregation. If these relationships are positive, the congregation will receive the pastor as a person of credibility, as someone in whom they can believe. Creating this positive feeling is as critical in preaching as it is in any form of communication (as, for example, the analogy of the ambassador cited earlier).

Every congregation or audience needs to know that the preacher or speaker is: (1) *competent;* that is, a person "who knows what he is talking about," (2) a person of *integrity;* that is, the speaker does not try to manipulate or exploit, but is a person who can be trusted, and (3) *vitality;* that is, the preacher communicates a deep sense of belief in all that is said. The identity by the congregation of the messenger as a credible source is critical in preaching. When credibility is present the congregation is free to respond, to interact with the message as well as the messenger. Without it, the preacher faces a congregation that is fettered by a lack of confidence in the messenger and therefore the message. The apostle Paul faced a credibility problem in Corinth. He did not appeal to the Corinthians to defend his reputation so that he would be received, but so that his message would be received. Paul based this plea on an appeal to his integrity: ". . . we are made manifest unto God; and I trust also are made manifest in your consciences" (II Cor. 5:11b). "Manifest" means literally, "to be turned inside out." This was Paul's way of saying, "I have no ulterior or suspicious motives. What you see is a man devoted to God's service. What you get is what you see."

This chapter has touched lightly on a theology of proclamation. It has looked at some of the complexities of communication as they affect preaching. One of the least difficult aspects of preaching is organizing delivery so that it supports content. The following chapters are devoted to the mechanics of sermon delivery that support content, thereby maximizing the message and minimizing the messenger.

2 Improving Full Vocal Production

"Anybody can talk."

The preacher had come to the point of application in the conclusion of his sermon. His words were incisive, and they were a direct appeal to non-Christians in the congregation. He said, "Do you know what you need? You need Jesus!" The content of his application was strong and accurate. Unfortunately, however, few people could understand what he said. This is because the question, "Do you know what you need?" was preached in a gravelly, strained, extremely high-pitched voice. He literally gave the question all of the vocal emphasis he could muster. Consequently, the answer to his question, "You need Jesus!" was vocalized in a rushed, hissing sound that I call the dramatic whisper. His most important words, "You need Jesus," were not understood by the only "lost" person in the congregation. The content was fine, but the delivery was a total failure.

The use of full vocal production could have helped that preacher communicate his message clearly and strongly. He was just forty-three years old at the time that sermon was preached, but he had been abusing his voice since his call to preach 18 years before. In fact, he thought that he *had* to strain his voice in order to sound like a preacher. Following this stereotype gave him a sore throat every Sunday, hoarseness on Monday, and permanent vocal damage by the time he was 46 years old. His faulty concept was fed, at least in part, by the notion that *what* he preached was less important than *how* he preached. These fallacies have attached themselves to preaching in a way that hinders the communication of the gospel and cripples the preacher's ability to speak. It usually occurs just at the time the preacher is entering the prime of ministerial life.

The purpose of this chapter is to explain the dynamics of full vocal production. Proper vocalization enables speakers to preserve and protect their voices. It also enables speakers to realize the full potential of their individual voice quality.

Proper vocalization is achieved by the use of full vocal production. There is nothing mysterious about this process. Full vocal production simply puts to use the parts of our bodies that God created for speaking. Full vocal production is usually referred to as diaphragmatic speaking. The term *full vocal production,* however, seems to me to be more descriptive of the proper vocalization process. Therefore, we will use that descriptive terminology in this book.

Diaphragmatic Breathing

Intrinsic to full vocal production is controlled, diaphragmatic breathing. (Most speech books refer to diaphragmatic breathing as respiration. However, respiration can also refer to breathing that is not diaphragmatic. Besides, I intend my terminology to be descriptive rather than technical.) The purpose of breathing, of course, is to supply oxygen to the body. The speech process makes use of this primary function. For that reason, speech is often described as a secondary or overlaid function.

Diaphragmatic breathing is breathing deeply enough to affect the diaphragm. The diaphragm is a thin band of muscle located in the upper abdominal area just beneath the lungs.

Figure 1

The diaphragm is tense and flat during inhalation, relaxed and dome-shaped at end of exhalation.

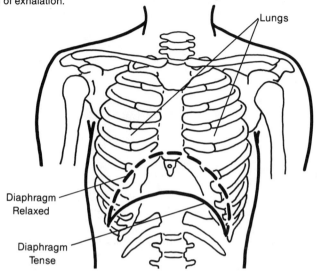

The diaphragm separates the chest (thoracic) cavity from the abdominal cavity. The diaphragm is shaped like a dome (actually a double dome) with the top of the dome rising toward the lungs. (See Figure 1.) As the lungs are filled with air (inhalation), they expand, pushing the diaphragm downward to an almost flattened position. The diaphragm, in turn, pushes the abdominal and rib muscles outward. Inhalation is now completed.

In the flat position the diaphragm is tense, much like a compressed spring. This tension is caused by the abdominal and rib muscles, which are returning to their original positions and applying pressure to the diaphragm. This tension compresses the lungs, increasing the air pressure in them. (See Figure 2.) This compression helps us exhale. (Controlling exhaling, as we will see, is important to full vocal production.) We need to note that in exhaling the diaphragm returns to its dome-shaped position, it remains relaxed until inhalation forces it downward again and the breathing cycle is repeated.

Figure 2

The downward movement of the diaphragm pushes abdominal muscles out-ward. The abdominal and intercostal muscles exert pressure on the diaphragm which exerts pressure on the lungs to bring about exhalation.

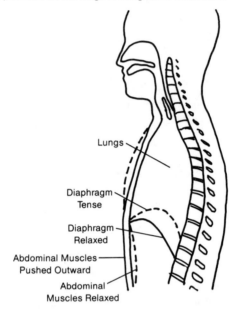

One can breathe without significantly affecting the diaphragm. This is known as shallow or clavicular breathing, because the collar bones and shoulder muscles rise while the abdominal and rib muscles barely move or do not move at all. Shallow breathing has the following devastating effects for the speaker: (1) It deprives the body of an adequate supply of oxygen. The lack of oxygen causes a rapid heartbeat, which compounds the tension the speaker naturally experiences. A sufficient supply of oxygen, on the other hand, helps the speaker relax. Without sufficient oxygen the body weakens, especially the legs. This is the reason nervous public speakers are often described as being "shaky in the knees." (2) The tension produced by shallow breathing is usually felt in the shoulders and throat, and it has a direct bearing on the throat and sinus cavities. The result is breathiness and a vocal pitch that is higher than normal. (3) As the speaker's sinus cavity closes from tension, breathing becomes even more difficult. As one experiences breathiness and hears an uncharacteristic stridency or high pitch in voice, a loss of self-confidence occurs. This in turn causes more tension, and the vicious circle continues until the speaker either relaxes or faints!

Diaphragmatic breathing not only helps the speaker develop the full potential of one's voice, it also gives one a way to control tension. All people feel tension or anxiety before they speak; often it is called "stage fright." In actuality, tension can be a useful servant of the speaker. When it is controlled by diaphragmatic breathing, it can be channeled into vitality in the speaker's delivery. (The specifics of channelling tension into vitality in delivery will be covered in chapters four and five.) The first steps toward making tension work for the speaker lie in acknowledging that tension is "natural" for all speakers, and that it can be modified by diaphragmatic breathing.

Exercises for Diaphragmatic Breathing

Two exercises are helpful in developing diaphragmatic breathing. Here is how to do them.

1. Stand up straight, but not rigidly. Place your hands on your sides just above your waist and just below your rib cage. Spread your fingers so that your thumbs point backward and your fingers point forward. Be sure your hands and fingers are touching your body, as if you were trying to wrap your hands around your waist. Inhale and exhale as normally as possible. Your hands should be moved outwardly as you inhale and then fall back toward your body as you exhale. (This will not be a large movement.) If the action is reversed or if you feel no movement, your breathing is too shallow. Repeat the process until your shoulders are relaxed and you are inhaling deeply enough to affect the diaphragm.

2. When you have mastered exercise one, add another step to the process. Inhale easily for about 5 seconds, then exhale

for 10 seconds. If you are out of breath in less than 10 seconds, you are exhaling too quickly. Repeat the exercise until you can control how quickly you exhale. Remember, controlling exhalation is critically important to full vocal production.

These two exercises are simple and basic, and there are many variations to them. For example, in the first exercise you could lie on your back on the floor or any hard surface with a book resting on your stomach. The book should rise slightly as you inhale and drop gently as you exhale. For exercise two you could make a hissing sound between your teeth so that you can hear how slowly and steadily you are exhaling. Some speakers and singers can sustain exhalation for 30 to 90 seconds. This helps them develop strength and versatility with their voices. You may also want to invent your own exercises. As with any exercise, you should first take the time to master the basics, then exercise regularly to maintain the fitness you have achieved.

Breathing for Speech

Breathing for speech calls for a simple but special control of the breathing process. Normal or nonspeech breathing is rhythmic: breathing for speech defies rhythm. Stevenson and Diehl have described breathing for speech as having "contrasting rhythm." "For metabolism it goes like this: Inhale through the nose (1-2-3); exhale through the nose (1-2-3). But in speech it should go like this: Inhale through the mouth (1); exhale through the mouth (1-2-3-4-5-6-7). Of course, in speech there is no exact mathematical ratio, but when a person is talking he has to inhale quickly and let the breath expire slowly and rather evenly while vibrating the vocal cords. Whereas breathing for metabolism is involuntary, breathing for speech has to be voluntarily controlled."[1]

Breathing for speech does not mean deep breathing. The

---

1. Dwight E. Stevenson and Charles F. Diehl, *Reaching People from the Pulpit* (New York: Harper and Row, 1958), pp. 40-41.

speaker should use no more breath in public speaking than one would in conversational speaking. Many speakers inhale noisily, either because they do not use diaphragmatic breathing or because they feel that noisy inhalation has some dramatic effect. In any speaking situation, some of the air that is inhaled will enter the lungs without any effort by the speaker. A basic law of physics helps the speaker inhale noiselessly. When the speaker pauses for breath, the air pressure in the speaker's body is slightly lower than it is outside the body. Higher air pressure always moves to lower air pressure. Some air, therefore, effortlessly moves into the speaker's lungs. The speaker, of course, must inhale to receive an adequate supply of air. Inhalation does not need to be deep, nor does it need to be noisy.

Jon Eisenson, in his superb speech book *Voice and Diction,* lists three objectives in breathing for speech: "(1) It should afford the speaker an adequate and comfortable supply of breath with the least awareness and expenditure of effort. (2) The respiratory cycle—inhalation and exhalation—should be accomplished easily, quickly, and without interference with the flow of utterance. (3) The second objective implies ease of control over the outgoing breath so that breathing and phrasing—the grouping of ideas—can be correlated functions."[2] These objectives are easily achieved by habitual diaphragmatic breathing.

Proper Vocalization

Full vocal production involves the coordinated activity of several muscles. As we have just seen, diaphragmatic breathing alone involves several muscles and organs. When a person exhales, air moves past the vocal bands. (See Figure 3.) Slight pressure on the vocal bands moves them closer together so that they resist the movement of air. This resistance causes the vocal bands to vibrate. (See Figure 4.) This vibration produces

---

2. Jon Eisenson, *Voice & Diction,* 3rd ed. (New York: Macmillan, 1974), p. 38.

Figure 3

Vocal bands are spread apart for breathing.

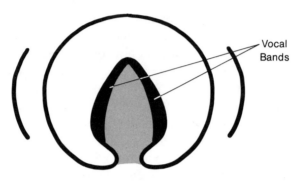

Figure 4

Vocal bands are closed for vocalization.

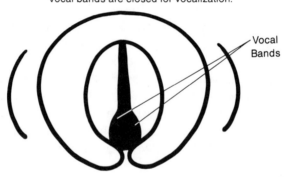

what is called voice (the technical term is *phonation*). Full vocal production provides a clear, strong voice without the effects of tension or strain.

Although the process of proper vocalization is not complicated, it is somewhat involved. The muscular coordination needed for full vocal production is much less complicated than would be needed for hitting a golf ball, riding a bicycle, swimming, or other enjoyable, beneficial activities. As with any muscular activity (as we saw with diaphragmatic breathing), full vocal production calls for intense concentration until the basic muscle movements are mastered. Then steady practice is required to maintain good coordination and muscular conditioning.

Vocalization occurs only during exhalation, never during inhalation. Let's follow an imaginary molecule of air through the entire vocalization process. A speaker inhales and the air molecule, along with millions of others, is drawn into the lungs. Various chemical changes take place inside the lungs as some oxygen is extracted from the molecule and delivered to the bloodstream. The air molecules are in constant motion, causing the lungs to expand. The diaphragm and muscles surrounding it are slightly displaced. Almost immediately, the muscles surrounding the diaphragm begin pushing back. The diaphragm transfers this pressure to the lungs. (We can temporarily stop this process by "holding our breath." When we hold our breath, we tighten our abdominal muscles so that they will not return to their relaxed position. This keeps them from exerting pressure on the diaphragm and the lungs.)

The abdominal and rib muscles will be in a hurry to return to their relaxed position. Our imaginary molecule of air will feel this pressure and will be ready for rapid expulsion from the lungs. The speaker who uses full vocal production, however, controls exhalation. This is achieved by controlling the amount of pressure the abdominal muscles are allowed to apply to the diaphragm and thus to the lungs. As the speaker regulates the amount of air that will vibrate his vocal bands, two things are accomplished: (1) the muscular tension for vocalizing is moved from the vocal bands (technically, the larynx) to the abdominal muscles; (2) as air outside the speaker is vibrated in the production of vocal sound, so the air inside the speaker's lungs is vibrated. This inner vibration reinforces the vocal sound by resonance from the chest cavity. (Full vocal production is not necessarily synonymous with a deeper voice.) Full vocal production relaxes the vocal bands and strengthens the voice by using the abdominal muscles to control exhalation (and, thereby, vocalization), and thus adds resonance to the voice.

Resonance is defined as the reverberation of any sound.

Vocal resonance, therefore, is the reverberation of the voice. Resonance is one of the two most important factors determining individual voice quality. The other is the structure of the vocal bands.

Vocal resonance is influenced by the bones of the head, the chest cavity, the throat cavity, and the nasal passages. The chest is the most powerful of all the resonators, and it is the one resonator that requires controlled muscular activity. The other resonators—head, throat, and sinus—influence the voice with little conscious effort. Chest resonance calls for the coordination of several muscular activities by the speaker.

So far, our imaginary molecule of air has been inhaled, forced into controlled pressure from the abdominal and rib muscles and the diaphragm, and vibrated by other molecules of air as they force their way past the vocal bands. Our molecule of air will also eventually find its way past the vocal bands. As it does it will assist in vibrating them for vocalization. Then it is expelled into the atmosphere to undergo a chemical change that will again make it viable for inhalation. Then the process is repeated. This process was summarized in a classic speech book as follows:

> The foundation of voice is the column of air that is forced out of the lungs by pressure of relaxed diaphragm and rib muscles, and the pressure of the viscera or abdominal organs against the diaphragm in exhaling. The air passes up through the larynx at the top of the windpipe. In the larynx are two muscular folds or bands that in quiet breathing form a V-shaped opening but that pull together when you cough or lift a heavy load. They also pull together when you wish to speak, so that the exhaled air is forced against them. These folds are commonly called the vocal cords—though vocal bands is a more accurately descriptive term. The air pressure vibrates these bands and produces sound waves. The tone thus produced passes through the pharynx (upper throat, where your tonsils are—or were) and the mouth, and, in the case of certain sounds, through the nose.

These cavities resonate the tone (literally re-sound it), amplify and enrich it.[3]

Vocalization is a combination of several muscular actions. These activities may appear to be involved, but most of them — breathing and vocalizing — are already in use by the speaker. Full vocal production simply adds proper coordination to these activities so that the speaker may preserve and protect the voice, and so that the speaker may develop the full potential of the individual voice.

Voice Quality

Voice quality is determined by the size and shape of the vocal bands, the size and shape of the vocal resonators, and by the speaker's perception of self. Voice quality is as individual as fingerprints. In fact, several court rulings across the United States have allowed voice print identification (spectograms) as evidence for identification. When the techniques of full vocal production are put into practice, the speaker can get an accurate "reading" of his/her individual voice quality.

The vocal bands are two narrow, tough strips of muscle tissue. They range in length from about ⅞ inch to 1 ¼ inches in adult men, and from about ½ inch to about ⅞ inch in adult women. The vocal bands are part of the "voice box" (larynx) at the front of the throat. They are housed inside a protective cartilage that causes a protrusion often referred to as the "Adam's apple." The vocal bands are connected in a V shape and lie flat within the larynx. (See Figure 3.) The opening between the vocal bands is called the glottis.

The length, thickness, and, to some extent, tension of the vocal bands determines voice quality. Short, thin vocal bands produce higher pitched sounds. Long thick vocal bands produce lower pitched sounds. (Too much tension also produces

3. Lew Sarett, William Trufant Foster, and Alma Johnson Sarett, *Basic Principles of Speech,* 3rd ed. (Boston: Houghton Mifflin Co., 1958), p. 212.

a higher pitched sound, but full vocal production transfers most of the tension from the vocal bands to the abdominal and rib muscles.) Once full vocal production is used, the speaker should not be concerned about making voice pitch lower. Full vocal production gives the speaker an optimum or "natural" pitch level. Optimum pitch is largely determined by the size of the vocal bands.

You can find your optimum pitch level in at least two ways. (1) Try the breathing exercise that calls for you to lie down with a book on your stomach. When you feel you are breathing diaphragmatically, try vocalizing the sound, "Ahhh." Be sure your throat muscles are relaxed. As your vocal bands vibrate, listen to this sound. It will be very close to your optimum pitch level. (2) Sing the musical scale, starting as low as you can and finishing the last note as high as you can. Your optimum pitch level will be at about the level in which you sang "fa, sol, la." The speaker should learn to be happy with that pitch level. Forcing the voice lower (retracting the voice) causes damage to the vocal bands. Once the speaker determines optimum pitch level, it should be accepted as his or her individual voice quality.

Vocalization occurs when the stream of breath under pressure forces the vocal bands apart. The vocal bands are far apart during breathing, and they are brought close together for vocalization. Air pressure builds beneath the vocal bands until they are forced apart. As the vocal bands are forced apart and air is allowed to pass between them, they vibrate, and vocalization occurs. If the air is constantly allowed to pass too quickly between the vocal bands, two negative results occur: (1) vocalization is breathy instead of resonant, and (2) the vocal bands become dry. Speaking when vocal bands are dry is much like driving an automobile without oil in the engine. Dryness causes friction, which does serious, possibly permanent, damage to the vocal bands. A drink of water gives only temporary relief. Full vocal production, with its strong control of exhalation, maintains the "natural" moisture within the larynx. Thus, the vocal bands are protected, and they are allowed to work at maximum efficiency.

The sound that results from the vibration of the vocal bands is reinforced by resonators. The resonators amplify and add further quality to the voice, much as the hollow box beneath the strings adds resonance to a violin. "Resonance gives to the voice greater volume, richness, and penetration: it gives tones a vibrant and bright quality."[4] Resonance occurs in the chest during vocalization, and it takes place in the other resonators just after vocalization. The resonators other than the chest are:

1. The upper throat cavity (pharynx). This is the soft muscular structure just above the larynx that opens into the nasal cavities and the mouth.

2. The nasal cavities, including the nose. Only the sounds *n, m,* and *ng* are resonated through the nasal cavity.

3. The mouth. Resonation from the mouth depends on how widely the mouth is opened during vocalization.

The size, shape, and general health of the resonators account for their differences in quality for individual speakers.

The way a speaker uses his or her voice can tell much about personality. Speaking (especially preaching) is, in part, an expression of the speaker's temperament. An intense speaker puts stronger emphasis on key words; a deliberate person speaks slowly; a cheerful person usually has a pleasant voice because there is no tension on the vocal bands; a person lacking self-confidence usually speaks in either a quiet voice or in a loud voice designed to disguise the lack of self-assurance; the "loner" tries to escape attention by speaking in a monotone; a domineering person speaks in a lofty, superior way. These are just a few of the psychological qualities of speaking, and they are admittedly oversimplified. Each of us may have several of these qualities, depending on our speaking situation.

We have already noted that preaching can be presumptuous. But we also noted that we presume to preach because we have

---

4. Sarrett, Foster, Sarrett, *Basic Principles,* p. 225.

been "called" to preach. Our self-confidence, then, does not come only from the authority of our own lives, but primarily from the authority of our calling. God has always been faithful to equip those whom He has called. We are constantly growing as Christians. We can add further direction to this growth by developing the use of full vocal production. This, in turn, will help us preach in a way that magnifies the message, but minimizes the messenger.

Exercises for Full Vocal Production

If we are to grow as Christians, we must make some investments. We can invest ourselves in full vocal production by doing a few basic exercises.

1. Standing straight but not rigidly, count from one to ten on one breath. Try to make your vocalization a little louder and stronger with each number. You may want to begin at a vocal level that is a little less than conversational tone. If you make it to ten on one breath, the last two or three numbers will involve effort from your entire body. (In fact you may be standing on your tiptoes on nine and ten!) If at any point you feel strain or soreness in your vocal bands, stop! Your voice is a delicate instrument that must never be strained.

Strain on the vocal bands means that you have not shifted the tension from your throat to the abdominal muscles. Concentrate on relaxing your throat muscles and tensing your abdominal muscles during vocalization.

2. Practice controlling exhalation while singing a hymn. Try to control your rate of exhale while singing so that when you come to a breath-stop in the hymn, you do not need to take a breath. This practice will help you learn to avoid exhaling too much air while speaking. Again, if you feel any vocal strain, stop! It is never advisable to strain your vocal bands.

3. If you cannot control exhaling from one breath-stop to another during a hymn, you need to develop some basic conditioning exercises. Consult a physician to determine whether you need to jog, ride a bicycle, or do some other exercise. The

overall fitness of a speaker is directly related to ability to communicate strongly and clearly.

Full vocal production is a simple process that requires proper muscular coordination. Using it will preserve and protect the speaker's voice. Many speakers have done serious and even permanent damage to their vocal bands because of years of vocal abuse. Many other speakers dread Sunday night services because their voices are still sore from their Sunday morning sermons. Some speakers begin to dread speaking at all—not because they don't enjoy speaking, but because they know it will hurt their throats. Other speakers try to compensate by retreating to dramatic whispers during the sermon or by depending too heavily on the amplification system. (What happens when the amplification system does not work? Besides, when we mumble into a microphone, the congregation simply hears an amplified mumble!) These practices are inexcusable. God has created us in a way that we can preach two, three, or even four times on Sunday without having a sore throat on Monday.

Full vocal production also helps a person develop the individual potential of his/her voice. A speaker's voice does not have to be, in fact should not be, gravelly and hoarse—unless there is a physiological problem. Speakers should have clear, strong voices, for they have a clear, strong message to proclaim. Most preachers would insist that they and their congregations should give their best to the Lord. Full vocal production is foundational for a speaker to give his/her best whenever (s)he speaks. Sermon delivery has been called ". . . the most dynamic moment of the preaching experience."[5] It is a shame that this "most dynamic moment" is often dreaded and then garbled by many speakers. Full vocal production can restore joy to speaking as well as add dynamism to this "most dynamic moment."

5. H. C. Brown, Jr., H. Gordon Clinard, and Jesse J. Northcutt, *Steps to the Sermon* (Nashville: Broadman Press, 1963), p. 164.

*When one who grew up with careless habits as to articula-
tion first attempts to correct them, he will for a while betray
the effort; but this can be soon overcome, by practicing exercises in private, and especially by care in conversation.*

John A. Broadus
*A Treatise on the Preparation
and Delivery of Sermons*

3 Improving Articulation

"Ah'm jist an ol' country boy."

After full vocal production is achieved, the next step in good speech is *articulation*. Full vocal production, as we have seen, is foundational to proper vocalization. Vocalization, however, is meaningless until it is shaped into sounds that communicate thoughts. This shaping process is called articulation. The articulated sounds are oral representations of the letters we use in writing.

American speech uses forty-four distinctive sounds. These individual sounds have the technical name "phonemes." Phonemes are the distinctive sound elements that, when combined in speech, comprise a word. The different phonemes, articulated correctly, help listeners distinguish words. For example, the word *God* has three distinct phonemes. Change the first phoneme to *s* and we have the word *sod*. Change the second phoneme to *a* and we have the word *Gad*. Change the last phoneme to *t* and we have the word *got*.

Clear articulation requires the relaxed, flexible, purposeful use of the lips, tongue, and jaw, and the meshing of individual sounds into combinations that form words. The phonemes of the word *God* are smoothly blended into one syllable, rather

41

than haltingly articulated as three isolated sounds. In addition, when we speak the sound of the last phoneme of an individual word is often blended into the first phoneme of the next word. When we say, "God is good," the phoneme *d* blends easily into the phoneme *i*. This process is called "elision." The elision between the phoneme *s* and the phoneme *g* in the sentence above is not so smooth as it was between *d* and *i*. Try saying aloud "God-is-good" by stopping the last sound of each word before beginning the first sound of the next word. Your speech will be halting and choppy. Elision provides smooth movement so that the individual words are articulated distinctly, but are also blended smoothly into the next word. (In the following chapter we will discuss how pauses are used to interrupt elision, as between sentences.) Clear articulation, therefore, requires distinctive phonemes eliding with each other in a way that enables the listener to distinguish the words being spoken.

When a preacher has clear articulation, it allows the congregation to relax and focus attention on the message. Poor articulation, however, hinders the communication process, because it forces the congregation to focus attention on deciphering sounds that have been misarticulated into meaningful words. Clear articulation makes listening easy for the congregation. Poor articulation makes listening difficult and transfers attention from the message to the messenger.

Speakers misarticulate in three major ways: (1) by substitution of sounds, such as "jist" for "just," "git" for "get"; (2) by omission of sounds, such as "preachin'" for "preaching," "gov'-ment" for "government"; (3) by addition of sounds, such as "warsh" for "wash," "athuhlete" for "athlete." Examples of misarticulation are legion. We could also mention "becuz" for "because," "wanna" for "want to," "gonna" for "going to," and "hunnert" for "hundred." Think of other misarticulated sounds you have heard. Make a list of the misarticulated sounds that are heard often, perhaps even from the pulpit.

Most misarticulated sounds are caused by a lazy use of the lips, tongue, and jaw. To verify this, try saying "jist" and then say "just"; say "git" and then say "get." Continue this exercise with the other examples of misarticulated sounds. In each case, notice that minimal additional effort is required to give fullness or clear articulation to these sounds. A failure to put forth this minimal effort produces lazy or poor articulation.

Some preachers, on the other hand, are overly precise with articulation. The laborious shaping of vowels and consonants also hinders communication, perhaps even more so than lazy speech habits. In either case the goal is to shape sounds in such a way that the congregation can hear the message without the distraction of either lazy or overly precise articulation.

The overall quality of speech, whether it be lazy, overly precise, or muffled, is known as *enunciation.* The words *enunciation, pronunciation,* and *articulation* are often used interchangeably. For our purposes *articulation,* as we have seen, refers to the shaping of individual sounds that comprise a word; *enunciation* refers to the overall quality of speech; and *pronunciation* refers to where the emphasis is placed within a word. For example, the word *insurance* could be pronounced "in´-surance" or "in-sur-ance."

It may be argued that some misarticulated sounds are accepted regional accents. In fact, some preachers justify lazy speech habits by saying it is a good way of "identifying with my people." Accents can enhance this identification, but lazy speech habits prohibit it. Many preachers take pride in their humility by claiming, "Ah'm jist an ol' country boy." Whether a speaker is from the country or city is immaterial. Lazy speech habits hinder clear communication, and a message from God's Word deserves to be communicated clearly.

Accents are related to both pronunciation and articulation and also include accepted varieties in the rate of speech: slow or fast. Accents represent what the general population accepts for speech in various regions of our country. For example, President Jimmy Carter's last name is often uttered rapidly and spoken as "Cotta" in the northeastern states; it is drawled as "Cahtuh" in the southern and southwestern states; and it is enunciated as "Carter" in the midwestern and western states. What is correct? The former President enunciated his last

name "Cahtuh," reflecting his Georgian speech pattern. It
could be argued that "Cahtuh" is the correct enunciation of his
name because that is the way he enunciates it. But someone
named Carter who lives in the midwest may prefer to sharpen
the *r* sounds and enunciate the name as "Carter." Would
"Carter" then be the proper enunciation of that name?

Establishing standards for enunciation would be nearly im-
possible in America. The individual speaker might never think
about the possibility that (s)he speaks with an accent unless
(s)he leaves the region where his/her pattern is accepted. A
person from the south, for example, who goes to the northeast
may be startled by the "accent" of the persons (s)he meets.
Then (s)he would be appalled at the number of persons who
told him *(s)he* has a funny accent. We must understand that
accents aren't accents until we leave the region where our
speech patterns are generally accepted.

The speaker who wishes to eradicate or modify an accent
needs to evaluate the way (s)he places emphases on syllables
and how (s)he articulates vowels and consonants. To cite a
previous example, is the word pronounced in-surance or
in-sur´-ance? Dictionaries are good guides for proper pronunciation. But dictionaries are dynamic tools, changing as the
accepted patterns of speech change. Be certain to use a recent
dictionary.

We have already seen how the consonant *r* can be variously
enunciated in the name Carter. Most accents, however, are
distinguished by the way vowels are articulated. The first
person pronoun actually has two sounds; long *i* and long *e*.
(See the phonetic articulation guide at the end of the chapter.)
A lazy speech pattern (which is also identifiable as part of a
regional accent), negates those two sounds by articulating the
first person pronouns as "ah." Other regional accents may
articulate both the long *i* and long *e* sounds, but will nasalize
the word. This is how a midwestern accent is identified. The
word *sin* usually has one syllable. But some regional accents
articulate the word as "si-yun," using two syllables.

How is the speaker to know when (s)he is speaking

correctly? The answer is not definitive, but the following steps will be helpful. 1. Check a recent dictionary for a pronunciation guide for individual words. 2. Be sensitive to generally accepted speech patterns in various regions of the nation. 3. Check the articulation guide in this chapter, to avoid lazy speech habits.

Accents lend color and flavor to speech. Speech would be monotonous without the variety that accents offer. So, be tolerant of the "accents" of others. Remember that all of us have an accent. We just do not know it is an accent until we leave our region of general acceptance for speech patterns.

Accents can be colorful, but lazy speech is a hindrance. A general articulation guide for the English language follows. Study the descriptions of the individual sounds, then say the practice words and sentences aloud. You will find it extremely helpful to practice on a tape recorder.

The International Phonetic Alphabet lists forty-four different speech sounds used in the English language. Most of these sounds are vocalized, but a few are not. Nonvocalized sounds do not vibrate the vocal bands. Regional variations make teaching these sounds difficult. The reader may have always heard words spoken with different sounds than indicated in the chart below. Nevertheless, the reader is offered each of the forty-four speech sounds, a concise description of how to form that sound in speech, and a few exercise words and sentences that use the individual sounds.[1]

General Articulation Guide

1. *Long a* as in pay. This sound is produced in the back of the mouth with the middle of the tongue arched and the lips spread slightly.

age   ray   danger

---

1. Jon Eisenson's superb book *Voice & Diction* offers a detailed description and practical exercises for every sound in the English language.

Amos made a plea for a return to the Lord.

The game was played as the evening turned gray.

2. *Short a* as in sat. The tongue is relaxed, arching the top downward. The sound is formed at the front of the mouth and the mouth opened wider than it was for *long a.* If the tongue is arched and this sound is made too far in the front of the mouth, *short a* will tend to be nasalized. This nasalized *short a* is standard speech in some parts of America.

hat   begat   Acts

Jesus sat and taught them, saying . . .

Andrew and Nathaniel had a visit.

3. *a* as in father. The tongue is arched in back, but otherwise is relaxed. The mouth is open wide as in *short a,* but the sound is formed in the back of the mouth.

calm   palm   ark

The father walked calmly through the dark.

What tall palm trees we saw!

4. *a* as in wall. The tongue is arched slightly higher than it was for father. The lips are rounded. The sound is formed in the back of the mouth.

5. *b* as in baptist. This sound is formed primarily with the lips. The lips are closed, but air behind the lips forces them open to release the vocalized sound. The explosive part of this sound is usually omitted when *b* is the last letter of the word, such as "comb."

bell   baptize   bless

Brother Bob bought a black suit.

Born again by the blood of the lamb.

6. *c* as in Corinth (identical with *k* as in kite and *q* as in

"quick"). This is a nonvocalized consonant. The tongue is firmly arched to the roof of the mouth. The sound is made as the tongue and soft palate are separated by the compression of air.

care   Caiaphas   calendar

Calvin commented because he cared.

Caleb called for consideration.

7. *ch* as in church. This sound is a combination of *t* and *sh* which we will study later. The front of the tongue is placed firmly on the front part (gum ridge) of the roof of the mouth. The sound is made as compressed air separates the tongue from the hard palate.

child   chore   chair

Choose to change from teaching to preaching.

The lunch was held in the orchard near the church.

8. *d* as in do. The top of the tongue is placed firmly against the gum ridge. As compressed air pushes the tongue away from the gum ridge, the sound is vocalized.

deacon   Didymus   deliver

The deacon declared his love for the Lord.

Thomas doubted at first but then confessed, "My Lord and my God."

9. *Long e* as in tree. The tongue is arched to the top, at the middle of the mouth. A little tension of the tongue and lips is required to produce this sound. This sound has various spellings, such as ski, believe.

Ezekiel   be   see

"See Him yonder on Calvary's tree."

Behold, He walks on the sea.

10. *Short e* as in let. The tongue is slightly arched in the center of the mouth, with little tongue or lip tension.

beget   set   den

"Lest we forget Gethsemane . . ."

We felt blessed when we met Him.

11. *f* as in favor. This sound is not vocalized and is produced by putting the lower lip against the upper teeth and forcing air between the lower lip and upper teeth.

fast   far   faith

The son left the father and headed for a far country.

Find the faith that sets you free.

12. *g* as in God. This sound is produced like the *c* (k, q), but there is less tension of the tongue against the palate.

Galatians   garden   Goshen

They gathered in the garden of Gethsemane.

The group grew in spirit and in grace.

13. *h* as in heaven. This is a nonvocalized consonant. This sound is dependent on the vowel that follows it for its articulation position. The sound is made in the throat almost as a whisper.

half   heard   Hezekiah

Hezekiah heard the prophet as one sent from heaven.

He hallowed the ground on which he humbly walked.

14. *Long i* as in idol. This sound is difficult to describe. It approximates the sound *a* as in father and *long e* as in he. The sound begins with the tongue in a slight arch and ends with the tongue in a firm arch. The first part of the sound is made in the back of the mouth; the second part is made toward the front of the mouth.

I   pride   Micah

I found the climb to be steep and high.

The light is my guide.

15. *Short i* as in wit. This sound is produced in similar manner as *long e,* but the tongue is more relaxed and is placed a little lower. The lips are also in a similar position as in the *long e* sound, but they are relaxed.

slip   in   bit

His wittiness lifted our spirits.

His limited speech was spoken quickly.

16. *j* as in Jesus. This sound is similar to *ch* except that it is vocalized, and less tension if placed on the tongue.

Joshua   jealous   Jeremiah

The crowd jostled Jeremiah just after he spoke.

Joshua jubilantly joined the battle.

17. *l* as in Lord. This is a vocalized consonant produced with the tip of the tongue touching the upper gum ridge. The *d* sound is produced in a similar way, but the *d* sound has a stop and the *l* sound is continuous. To accomplish this, the center of the tongue is lowered to allow vocalized breath to pass over the sides of the tongue.

letter   learn   low

The letter to the churches was a revelation.

The Lord revealed Himself to the lonely group.

18. *m* as in man. This is a vocalized and nasalized sound. The lips are touching, but relaxed rather than pressed together. The teeth are slightly parted, and the tongue rests at the bottom of the mouth. The vocalized sound moves through the nasal passages.

Malachi   Matthew   member

The members made a major contribution.

We must remember the meaning of the message.

19. *n* as in neighbor. This is the second of three vocalized and nasalized sounds. The top of the tongue is placed firmly but not rigidly against the gum ridge. The vocalized sound moves through the nasal passages.

Noah   near   new

Notice that the new book is near your hand.

Noah knew that God had sent the rain.

20. *ng* (or *ing*) as in preaching. This is the third of three vocalized and nasalized sounds. The back of the tongue is arched and in contact with the soft palate. The vocalized sound moves through the nasal passages.

singing   praying   bring

He was going to bring a rousing sermon.

Sing a new song of the things which have come to pass.

21. *Long o* as in chosen. The back of the tongue is arched slightly and the lips are rounded.

owe   Obadiah   Romans

Don't you know how the song goes?

Moses wrote some of our oldest books.

22. *Short o* as in cross. The back of the tongue is arched sightly, but is more relaxed than in the *long o* sound. The lips are only slightly rounded.

lost   soft   wrong

The cost of the office was lost.

He picked up the cloth at the foot of the cross.

23. *oo* as in doom. This sound is produced with the tongue flattened and the lips rounded. It is a vocalized sound.

room   soon   pool

The book tells of a good man sitting beside the pool.

At noon the world shook and took them by surprise.

24. *p* as in Peter. The lips are closed, and compressed air behind the lips forces them apart to produce this non-vocalized sound. The lips are much more tense than in the *b* sound.

presence   hyper   Egypt

His parents took him from Palestine to Egypt.

Peter departed to be alone as he wept.

25. *r* as in religion. This sound can be produced in two ways: with the tip of the tongue arched to the roof of the mouth well behind the gum ridge, or with the center of the tongue arched to the roof of the mouth.

revelation   reverence   career

The preacher rested as he leaned on the rostrum.

The fund raising occurred in October.

26. *s* as in savior. This is a precise sound that can be distorted easily into a whistling or hissing sound. It can also be made into a sluggish *sh* sound. It is formed by several articulatory procedures:

1. The sides of the tongue are raised and pressed firmly against the inside of the back teeth.
2. The center of the tongue is lowered at midline, forming a groove.
3. The top of the tongue is placed behind but not touching the backs of the upper teeth.
4. There is a slight space between the rows of teeth.
5. Air is forced along the groove of the tongue toward the teeth.

6. The *s* is a voiceless consonant.

Sunday   sabbath   sermon

After Saturday comes Sunday.

Sermons are sources of inspiration.

27. *sh* as in shield. The tongue is flat, and air is forced over the tongue and through the opening between the rows of teeth. The lips are slightly rounded.

shallow   should   share

The child should share the sherbet.

Shallow sermons do not have sharp points.

28. *t* as in Titus. The tip of the tongue is raised and pressed against the top of the gum ridge. The front of the sides of the tongue are pressed against the upper back teeth. The sound is made as compressed air forces the tongue away from the teeth.

territory   terror   table

The twelve sat at the table.

Two departed and ten were left.

29. *th* as in thanks. The tip of the tongue is placed between the teeth. Breath is forced between the tongue and teeth to make this voiceless sound.

Thessalonians   thanks   thimble

Thanks be to the Thessalonians.

The thimble is over there.

30. *th* as in bathe. This sound is the same as the *th* above, except that it is vocalized.

soothe   scathe   either

We loathe the scathing sermon.

He seethed as he bathed in cold water.

31. *Long u* as in universe. The center of the tongue is arched to the roof of the mouth. The tongue moves to a flattened position as vocalized air moves past it. The lips are slightly rounded.

music   mute   humor

The music was heard on cue.

Humor in the Bible is unique.

32. *Short u* as in usher. The tongue is relaxed, but the center is arched a little and the mouth is open without rounding the lips.

under   utter   asunder

Under the leadership of Ahab, the nation suffered.

The city was utterly destroyed and torn asunder.

33. *v* as in victory. The *v* is produced as the *f,* with these exceptions: the *v* is voiced and is produced with less air pressure.

valid   visit   veil

The veil of the temple was divided.

It is valid to make a pastoral visit.

34. *w* as in will. This sound has two movements: initially, the lips are rounded in pursed position but not touching the teeth. The tongue is arched in the center against the soft palate. The lips spread slightly at the end of the sound. This is a vocalized sound.

wisdom   was   winsome

It was his will that he speak wisely.

The winsome widow seemed aware.

35. *wh* as in whither. This sound is produced just as the *w* is produced, except *wh* is not vocalized.

where   which   whether

When you decide whether to go, let us know where.

Which do you prefer, white or blue?

36. *y* as in yield. The center of the tongue is arched toward the front of the mouth against the hard palate, and the lips are spread slightly—almost in a smile. This is a vocalized sound.

yesterday   yes   yonder

Yom Kippur was observed yesterday.

Yes, you may yield.

37. *z* as in zealot. This sound is produced in the same way as the *s* sound, except the *z* is vocalized and the *s* is not. The *z* is produced with less tension on the tongue than is the *s*.

zoo   Zacchaeus   Zipporah

Zipporah felt Moses was zealous.

Zacchaeus seized the opportunity.

38. *zh* as in treasure. *zh* is produced in the same way as *sh,* except that the *zh* sound is vocalized.

azure   brazier   seizure

The seizure occurred under the azure sky.

The treasured writing was thrown into the brazier.

39. *dzh* as in wages. This sound is similar to the *ch* sound, except that it is vocalized.

wages   ages   stage

The stage was set for Jonah.

The wages of love last for ages.

40. *a* as in task. This sound is placed after the others because it is rarely distinguished in American speech.

Because of its regional quality, I recommend you master this sound only if you plan to work in the New England area, or in areas where the spoken English bears a British influence. This sound is between the *a* sound of sat and the *a* sound of father.

Because of regional differences, any word exercises here may not be distinguishable to some regional speech patterns. Therefore, they are not included in examples 40-42.

41. *o* as in coffin. This is another regional sound that is not generally distinguished in America. This sound is produced just as the short *o,* except the lips are rounded.

42. *er* and *ir* sound. There are a variety of regional practices for producing this sound. For some speakers, the *r* sound suffices, for other speakers there is a distinctiveness between the *r* sound and the *er-ir* sound. This sound is produced in similar fashion as the *r* sound except that a little more tension is put on the tongue, and the lips are not rounded.

43. *ou* as in thousand. This continuous sound is generally produced with the tongue arched to the back of the soft palate. The lips are spread slightly and move to a rounded position.

rouse   pout   round

The round man was aroused to anger.

A thousand soldiers were routed in battle.

44. *oi* as in soil. this is a combination of the sound for *o* as in coffin and the *long e* sound as in tree. It is a continuous vocalized sound.

turmoil   avoid   toil

They toiled in the oil fields.

The turmoil was avoided.

A careful study and practice of the sounds indicated here will help the speaker improve articulation. The benefits will be more clear and therefore more easily understood speech, enabling the audience to concentrate on the message, not the messenger.

I have heard of a brother who in his earlier days was most acceptable, but who afterwards dropped far behind in the race because he by degrees fell into bad habits: he spoke with a discordant whine . . . and used such extraordinary mouthings that people could not hear him with pleasure. He developed into a man to be esteemed and honored, but not to be listened to. . . .

Doubtless, faults in even so secondary a matter as posture have prejudiced men's minds, and so injured the success of what would otherwise have been most acceptable ministries.

Spurgeon
Lectures to My Students

4 Improving Vocal Variables
"But what are you really saying?"

An elementary rule of communications states that a speaker's emotional message is more quickly conveyed than the intellectual message. The emotional message involves the feelings—authority, love, resentment, and others. The intellectual message involves the words used to communicate the message. The intellectual message deals directly with language, while the emotional message is sometimes categorized in a vague field of study called "paralanguage."

In preaching, the ideal is for the emotional message to support the intellectual message. The relation between the two can be illustrated by the various uses of the word *no.* We can say "no" tentatively in a way that says, "Keep on asking and I will change my response." We can also say "no" thoughtfully in a way that says, "I am not totally convinced that my response is correct. I am open to new information." Or we can say "no" obligingly in a way that says, "I don't want to say no, but I feel I must." And, we can say "no" definitely in a way that says, "My negative answer is final!" The intellectual message remained the same in each response, but the emotional message was completely different in each case.

Communication experts do not agree about what constitutes paralanguage, nor about what we have referred to as the emotional message.[1] Some scholars include only the *vocal variables*—pitch, volume, rate, and pause. Other scholars would include only body language—posture, gestures, facial expressions, and personal appearance. Since both the vocal variables and body language are intrinsically involved in effective communication, we will include both of them in this brief study of paralanguage and how it relates to speaking.

Vocal Variables

We will consider each of the vocal variables in speaking: pitch, volume, rate, and pauses.

Pitch

The first vocal variable, *pitch,* refers to the tonal qualities produced in vocalization. As we saw in chapter two, vocalization is produced as a controlled breath is exhaled past the vocal bands and vibrates them. All vocalization is produced at various pitch levels, ranging from high to low. Five factors need to be understood in our study of pitch: optimum pitch, pitch range, pitch interval, pitch intonation, and pitch inflection.

1. *Optimum pitch* was discussed in chapter two. The optimum pitch level is to be used as the median level from which higher and lower pitch levels are developed by the speaker.

2. *Pitch range* refers to the span between a speaker's highest and lowest pitch levels. A wider pitch range, used with effect

---

1. For a brief review of the problem, see David Crystal's essay "Paralinguistics," in *The Body As a Medium of Expression,* ed. Jonathan Benthall and Ted Polhemus (New York: Dutton, 1975), pp. 163-174.

to support content, gives a speaker flexibility and enhances appeal to an audience or congregation.

3. *Pitch interval* refers to the distance between two consecutive pitch levels. A change in pitch level can occur between two words or within one word. A pitch interval within a word is often heard in the word *welcome*. The first syllable is usually said a little higher than the second if the speaker wants to communicate warmth and enthusiasm. If a speaker wanted to be formal in saying "welcome," each syllable would be uttered at the same low pitch level. No pitch interval would occur.

Pitch intervals between words can be experienced in quoting the first five words of Psalm 23:1. "The LORD is my shepherd. . . ." With a pitch interval between "the" and "Lord," the word *Lord* stands out.

4. *Pitch intonation* refers to the pitch range used within a certain group of words such as a phrase or a sentence. If pitch intonation repeats itself frequently, a pattern can be easily detected. We will look at several examples of intonation problems, including a monotonous pattern, later in this chapter.

5. *Pitch inflection* refers to the movement from one pitch level to another within a syllable or a word. Use of inflection was illustrated in the opening paragraph of this chapter, when several uses of the word *no* were given. Varieties in pitch inflection were used to modify the emotional message.

Pitch patterns involve predictable ways of inflecting or intoning a sentence. One of these ways has become known as "the ministerial tone." I find it so offensive, however, that I've decided to call it "the ministerial whine." This pitch pattern can easily be illustrated. (See Figure 5. Here we need a machine that has not been invented. This machine would follow the same principle as an electrocardiogram, which measures the depth and rhythm of the heart beat. This machine would type the words of our sermon and record the pitch variations used with the individual words. In lieu of this un-invented machine, I submit a rough sketch.) The horizontal line indicates the range of pitch. Notice the definite pattern of the ministerial whine.

Figure 5

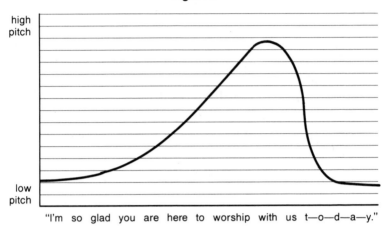

"I'm so glad you are here to worship with us t—o—d—a—y."

Figure 6

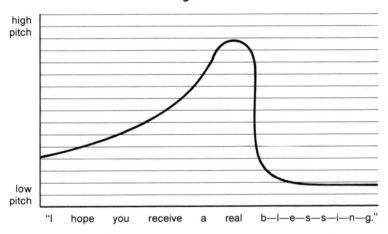

"I hope you receive a real b—l—e—s—s—i—n—g."

Multiply this pattern over hundreds of sentences in a thirty-minute sermon, and you can easily realize why a rescue mission congregation would turn down a warm meal rather than endure a sermon preached in ministerial whine.

Another pitch pattern problem for preachers involves the last few words of sentences. In this pattern the concluding words are spoken with a predictable drop in pitch. (See Figure 6.) This is usually done for two reasons: (1) to let the

Figure 7

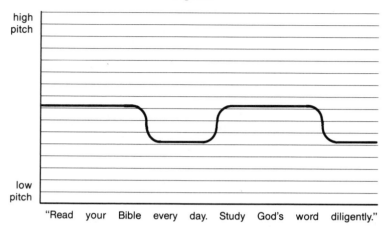

"Read your Bible every day. Study God's word diligently."

congregation hear the period they cannot see, and (2) because the speaker is thinking about the next sentence and subconsciously allows the energy level to drop. Such preoccupation causes the pitch pattern to look like this (see Figure 7).

How can monotonous pitch patterns be avoided? By relating the use of pitch to content! One practical and beneficial way of relating pitch (or any vocal variable) to content is to prepare a transcript of a recent sermon from a tape recording. A transcript differs from a manuscript in that it is a copy of what has actually been said, whereas a manuscript is a copy of what was planned to be said. Copy the sermon word for word from a tape recording. Be honest in transcribing. When "git" is said in, "Git thee behind me, Satan," then transcribe it g-i-t.

This transcript will enable the speaker to see and hear the sermon simultaneously.[2] Listen for pitch patterns. When they are detected, stop the tape. Use the transcript to say the same words aloud, this time striving to relate pitch to content. You

2. An initial shock will occur at seeing the sermon in writing. Remember, oral and written styles differ. However, the transcript may reveal a need for further work in clarity of diction. For instance, one of my transcripts revealed an eighty-two word sentence! An important side benefit of the transcript is that it drives us to clearer thought patterns.

Figure 8

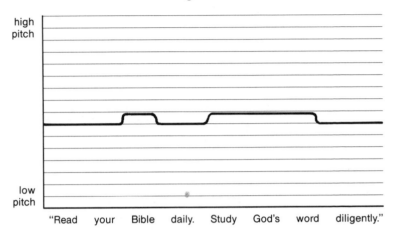

may need to experiment several times. Further exercises for all of the vocal variables will be discussed in chapter five.

The use of a transcript has been the single most quickly corrective exercise I have ever used to improve both content and delivery. The tediousness of transcription repays itself richly with the excitement of discovering ways to improve delivery immediately. The transcript approach is time-consuming and humbling. After the first exercise, it may be sufficient to transcribe only a few paragraphs rather than the entire sermon. Remember, your goal is to use pitch in a way that supports your content.

Some preachers have the problem of using only a narrow range of pitch. When this occurs, all words tend to sound alike. Because the transitions and descriptions do not stand out, the congregation has difficulty following the message. The narrow pitch range may be graphed in this way (see Figure 8).

Preachers who have a narrow pitch range usually think they are using a much wider range, and they feel their message is being communicated clearly. Often such speakers feel that if they use a wider pitch range they will be too demonstrative or dramatic.

To solve this problem, the speaker may need to do a little

psychological reconditioning. One way to accomplish this is to use a practice tape recording in which the speaker uses a much wider variety in pitch than would ordinarily be used in oral communication. The purpose of this exercise is to remove the inhibitions that limit the use of effective variety in pitch. For the inhibited speaker, a good communicative pitch range may "feel" demonstrative and dramatic. By exaggerating the use of pitch, one may open the door to effective changes in speaking. Emphasize variety in the use of pitch inflection.

The process goes something like this: Listen to a portion of a recent sermon while looking at its transcript. Then turn the recorder off and reiterate the same words, using exaggerated variety in pitch. Repeat the exercise, then record on another tape the same portion of transcript while striving to use a wider, more effective range of pitch. Finally compare the practice tape with the sermon tape. Repeat the exercise until you feel comfortable with using effective variety in pitch.

Volume

Volume refers to the amount of force needed in speaking for the message to be heard, and for the emotional message of the sermon to be conveyed. Preachers have had the same problems with volume as they have had with pitch: monotonous patterns and narrow range.

The excessive volume patterns among preachers have been caused by the fallacy that preaching is suspect unless it is loud. The cure is to realize that volume is a servant of content. The speaker should therefore use force or abstain from it as content dictates. Two typical volume patterns appear. This graph represents what happens when volume is up at the beginning of a sentence and down at the end (see Figure 9).

The second common volume pattern occurs because the preacher's energy lags behind a mistaken ambition to shout throughout the sermon. This graph illustrates the use of volume through the entire sermon (see Figure 10).

If one had the physical strength to do so, such a preacher would use a volume range limited to the upper levels. The

Figure 9

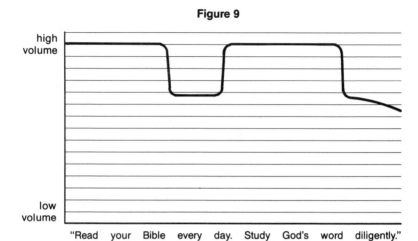

"Read　your　Bible　every　day.　Study　God's　word　diligently."

Figure 10

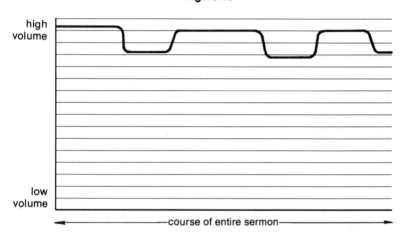

dubious goal would be to have volume level at the top of the scale throughout the sermon, and the graph would look like this (see Figure 11).

Note that this volume range indicates that all of the content should receive equal emphasis. Pragmatically, that means that illustrations would sound as emphatic as key theological assertions. Imagine a preacher saying in a thundering voice, "JESUS

Figure 11

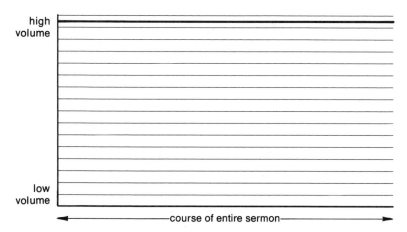

HONORS THE FAITH OF A REPENTANT SINNER!" That may be worth shouting about. But if this shouting preacher is to meet the goal, "THAT REMINDS ME OF THE TIME I WAS A LITTLE BOY!" must also be said in a thundering voice. The theological assertion and the personal illustration, according to this preacher's use of volume, are of equal importance. The illustration, of course, is not so important as the theological assertion, and should be given less emphasis by the use of a lower volume level. In that way, volume supports content.

Some preachers react to this approach by a determined effort to avoid "preacherly" high volume. They are prone to make the same mistake, however, by using volume in a narrow, low range and again without strong relationship to content. Their use of volume is easily graphed (see Figure 12).

Many preachers use volume in a narrow but medium range that also does not relate strongly to content (see Figure 13).

When pitch and volume are used effectively to support content, graphing is without pattern and difficult to illustrate.

Again, it helps to prepare a transcript of a recent sermon. Achieve variety in volume much the same way you practiced achieving variety in pitch; exaggerate the use of higher or lower volume as needed.

Figure 12

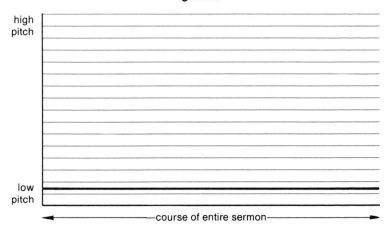

Figure 13

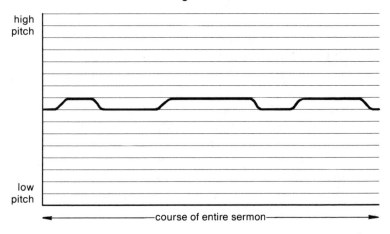

Rate

Rate refers to the speed at which a person speaks. Rate is misused in three ways: the speaker talks too fast, too slow, or at the same rate throughout. The best way to use rate for good communication is to be flexible. The needs of content should determine the amount of variance. Faster rates may be used for the less important details; slower rates for key assertions and ideas. A very slow, deliberate rate, with a minimum of elision, is used to give very strong emphasis.

Preachers often insist that they must speak rapidly in order to communicate excitement. Rapid rate is only one way, and not necessarily the best way, to achieve that goal. All of the vocal variables, as well as the use of body language, should work together to communicate varying levels of excitement.

Some preachers insist that it is "natural" for them to speak rapidly. They aren't sure what constitutes this driving force; however, they are sure they do not feel like challenging it. But note that in both instances the misuse of rate calls attention to the messenger rather than the message. The purpose of speaking is hampered when the audience notices how fast the preacher is talking. Rather than becoming a servant to speech rate, the speaker should make it serve him/her.

Several good exercises can help control rate. Reading aloud the poetry of either Walt Whitman or Robert Frost virtually defies rapid speech. Care must be taken to paint the same oral pictures they have drawn verbally. Even so, the rate will vary. Examine the following excerpt from "Drumbeat" by Whitman.[3]

Slow, emphatic:	beat! beat! drums!
	blow! bugles! blow!
Slightly faster:	Through the windows—through doors—
	burst like a ruthless force,
	Into the solemn church
	and scatter the congregation,
	Into the school where the scholar
	is studying. . . .

Try this passage from Scripture:

Slow:	'Saul, Saul
Moderate:	Why are you persecuting me?'
Fast:	And he said,

3. *Walt Whitman's Poems,* ed. Gay Wilson Allen and Charles T. Davis (Washington Square, New York: New York University Press, 1955), p. 200.

Slow:	'Who art thou, Lord?'
Fast:	And He said,
Moderate:	'I am Jesus whom you are persecuting,'

Rate has many variations. "Slow," "moderate," and "fast" are merely guidelines. Most people use a wide variety of rate in normal conversation, but they tend to become inhibited in public speaking and speak at the same pace.

The best method for correcting problems in rate has already been prescribed. Examine the transcript of a recent sermon while listening to it on tape. As you look at each sentence of the sermon, ask why that particular rate was used. Select key passages in the transcript and experiment with a variety of rate levels. Determine which is best for that particular passage.

As a basis for self-testing, think of 125-150 words per minute as average. This pace allows little room for variety. From this average you can increase your variety; a little faster than 150 words per minute at times when sermon content does not require special emphasis and a little slower than 125 words per minute when sermon content does require emphasis. Consider a few excerpts from the sermon, "The Prophetic Ministry," by G. Earl Guinn.[4] The opening paragraph may be read at 100-125 words per minute:

> When our ancestors were drinking blood out of the skulls of their forefathers on the shores of the Baltic Sea, China and India were ancient civilizations. They were religious countries then, and they are the same today. Their cultures have been more or less static and constant. In many respects they were not unlike the ancient Egyptians, Persians and Hebrews. They took worship seriously, even to the point of sacrificing their offspring to their deities. Now our Western civilization and culture stand aghast at the fiendish fetishes of the ancient rites. We have differing standards and concepts of values. Whence came this difference? For the most part the difference is due to the views and efforts of the prophets of Israel. Never in the history of the

4. *Southern Baptist Preaching,* ed. H. C. Brown, Jr. (Nashville: Broadman Press, 1959), pp. 87-95.

race have so many owed so much to so few. Jesus was in the line and tradition of the Hebrew prophets, although far more than a prophet. To the Christian he is Son of God and Redeemer. Yet many of his pronouncements were prophetic. He came not to destroy the law and the prophets but to vindicate, enrich, and make complete.

The last paragraph of the introduction might call for a slightly faster rate—perhaps 125-150 words per minute:

In the Boston public library there is an impressive painting by John S. Sargent showing these men as living characters. It would be helpful if every preacher had a copy of this painting hanging on the wall of memory to remind him always that his primary task is the preaching of God's truth. There is a call today for the prophetic type of ministry.

The conclusion to this sermon is a crescendo, and it defies rapid rate. Each sentence is an assertion that must be emphasized. Read a portion of that conclusion aloud, timing yourself as you do. Try for a rate of 90-110 words per minute.

Listen, men of God! Are you in his will and cooperating with his purpose? Are you serving his cause and preaching his grace? Then stop worrying about your opposition and pay no attention to their looks. God Almighty is marching on. He who notices every sparrow's fall and holds the whole wide world in his hand will never leave thee nor forsake thee. Let the heathen rage and the wicked imagine a vain thing. He will have them in derision. He that sitteth in the heavens shall laugh.

God is not a God of unfinished business. Victory belongs to our God. We are not on a sinking ship. We follow not a blind leader. We serve not a puny God. He sees the end from the beginning, and we need not fear to enter any door to which God holds the key.

This is not a call to complacency but a battle cry. Our God is moving. Let us move with him to victory and immortality, toward the great and terrible day of the Lord.

Remember, use variety in rate in a way that supports content, and not in a way that calls attention to the speaker.

Pauses

Rate and *pauses* work together. When rate and pauses are discussed together, they are usually known as phrasing. In oral communication, a phrase is a group of words expressing a thought. These phrases are separated and at the same time interlocked by pauses. To communicate our message effectively, we must use pauses in a variety of ways.

Brief pauses are used to allow the listener time to absorb what is heard. Longer pauses usually indicate a change of thought, but they may also be used to gain attention. Intermediate pauses may be used to introduce or dismiss a related but extraneous idea, to make a transition from one thought to another, or to allow time for descriptive material to be absorbed. Follow this general guideline: a brief pause is about one second or less in length; an intermediate pause is one to two seconds in length; a long pause is three to five seconds in length or longer. As with rate, there are many options for the lengths of pauses. Consider a few examples:

Matthew 5:13 calls for use of shorter pauses because of the relatedness of the material: "You are the salt of the earth;" (short pause) "but if the salt has become tasteless," (intermediate pause) "how will it be made salty again?" (short pause) "It is good for nothing any more," (short pause) "except to be thrown out and trampled under foot by men" (NASB).

Long pauses are most often used to indicate a change of thought. They are also good devices for gaining attention. The lengthy silence (lengthy, that is, when compared to the brief and intermediate pauses that are used a majority of the time in preaching) draws attention to itself and thus to the next few words you preach. Use a pause for this purpose infrequently, and only when you have something very important to say. As your sermon progresses, you may need an occasional long pause when you move from one point or section to another.

The long pause allows time for information to be digested, and it communicates the fact that a major shift in ideas is taking place. Consider an excerpt from the sermon "The Gospel of Isaiah" by Herschel H. Hobbs.[5] The first point is: The Gospel Concerning Sin. The second point is: The Gospel Concerning Suffering. Note the need for a pause:

> It is in this light that Isaiah regards man. This is the message of the gospel concerning sin. (Intermediate to long pause, perhaps two to three seconds).
> Every moment we live testifies to the truth that sin produces suffering.

Intermediate pauses have numerous uses and are of varying lengths, depending on the demands of content. When Jesus said: "Behold, there went out a sower . . . ," an intermediate pause is needed after "Behold." The word *behold* means, "let me have your attention," or "listen to this." In this instance, an intermediate pause allows time for attention to be focused on the words that follow. A similar pause may be used to introduce a quotation. For instance, "His mother said, Whatsoever he saith unto you, do it" (John 2:5). The intermediate pause is needed between "said" and "Whatsoever" to indicate that the quotation is about to begin. Intermediate pauses are also effective at the end of assertions or quotations, because they allow time for the congregation to absorb the message.

Vocalized pauses are popular, and that is unfortunate. Devices such as "uh" and "er" and sometimes "yuh know" communicate a feeling of uncertainty. A few vocalized pauses may be acceptable to most congregations, but they carry no intellectual message and they diminish your sense of authority or credibility. Be especially aware that vocalized pauses can become an unconscious habit—unconscious, that is, to the speaker. The congregation will notice them quickly. I once counted eighty-two "uhs" in one twenty-minute sermon. Do

5. Ibid., pp. 98-103.

not be afraid of a silent pause; a silent pause is much more effective than a nonsensical vocalized pause.

Volume, pitch, pauses, and rate are all servants of content. When these vocal variables are not used in a way that supports content, they call attention to themselves. This impedes the effective communication of the sermon. Effective use of full vocal production and the use of vocal variables in a way that supports content, emphasizes the message rather than the messenger.

Body Language

Nonverbal communication, more popularly referred to as *body language,* includes these factors: personal appearance, perceptions gained by the congregation in their first impressions of the speaker, walking to the pulpit or lectern, eye contact, facial expressions, posture, and gestures. These visible communication signals either support or hinder the message being expressed through language and voice. On some occasions, body language communicates a message without a word being said.

We would have difficulty communicating through language and vocal expressions alone. Try speaking without body movements. The vocal variables will tend to be flat or in a narrow range. This will be true whether you suppress gestures by making your body tight and rigid, or by making it extremely relaxed. *The communicative act requires the use of the total body.* The act of communication will rarely depend solely on the speech and breathing mechanisms.

The listener has difficulty receiving a message if he is not involved with the speaker. Body language helps a preacher induce a sense of empathy. Notice how football fans tense their bodies and push as if they were actually carrying the football those last few yards into the end zone. A speaker may communicate a sense of urgency, intensity, resignation, or excitement, by the use of body language. Such involvement with the speaker enhances the impact the message has on a listener.

"Whenever an audience participates with the speaker, feels in with him, yields to his movements, the speaker is well on the way toward achieving his purpose."[6] Preaching is definitely augmented by the use of body language. Listeners are much more likely to respond to a message from a person with whom they are involved. Body language that supports content dramatically helps produce that involvement.

Personal Appearance

The role of personal appearance in the communication process will never be known exactly. Too many variables occur in the tastes, subcultures, generation gaps, and individual idiosyncracies that shape the way a listener perceives a mode of dress. "We do know, however, that appearance and dress are part of the total nonverbal stimuli which influence interpersonal responses—and under some conditions they are primary determiners of such responses."[7]

The only general rule to apply regarding appearance is sensitivity. The speaker should dress for the occasion, whether it be informal, formal, or somewhere in between. The goal should be to dress in a way that does not distract the congregation from the message. A speaker can be distracting both by overdressing (too many colors, too formal for the occasion) and by underdressing (too informal for the occasion). The speaker should ask, "How will my personal appearance affect the way my congregation perceives of me as a person?" There may be no single accurate answer, but these considerations may minimize possible distractions.

First Impressions

Actually, personal appearance plays a significant role in developing a first impression. Beyond that, however, the congregation will also judge the potential of a speaker by personal

---

6. Sarrett, Foster, Sarrett, *Basic Principles,* p. 313.
7. Mark L. Knapp, *Nonverbal Communication in Human Interaction* (New York: Holt, Rinehart & Winston, 1972), pp. 85-86.

grooming, by the way the speaker meets other people, and by how comfortable one appears to feel about the speaking opportunity. The speaker's goal is to communicate a sense of self-assurance and ease that falls well short of arrogance but well above self-rejection.

Walking to the Pulpit

Listeners continue to gather impressions as they observe the way the speaker approaches the moment of delivery. The congregation has already been responding to the cues the speaker gives through personal appearance. This impression can be either affirmed or denied by the walk to the pulpit. The preacher's goal is to communicate alertness, self-confidence, and eagerness to share a message.

Take note of how people walk toward something that interests them. They do not walk on their toes, they do not slouch, they are not rigid. A natural movement to the pulpit will inform the congregation that you are comfortable and happy to be their speaker. (Consequently, it is not necessary to open the sermon with mundane remarks such as, "I am so happy to be here today," nor is it necessary to begin with an amusing anecdote that serves no purpose in that particular speaking situation.)

Heed this related piece of advice: do not speak before reaching the pulpit. The speaker should be established at the pulpit or lectern before one word is said.

Eye Contact

Make eye contact immediately. This is an excellent way for the speaker to become established at the pulpit before the first words are uttered. Eye contact may also be the last step in first impressions. Three major concerns about eye contact should be observed:

1. Establish eye contact before you speak the first words. Look toward the eyes of the congregation. There is no need to "nail" anyone with an intense gaze. A number of persons will feel as if you are looking directly at them if you look in their

general vicinity. Do not look over the heads of the congregation. Look directly at the people, and without moving too rapidly, establish eye contact with most if not all of them.

2. Maintain eye contact for 75 to 90 percent of the sermon or speech. You should be so familiar with your notes or manuscript that there is no obvious dependence on them. Never look down at your notes during or at the end of a key statement. Maintain eye contact during these important moments, and glance at notes during the pause after the statement is completed.

3. Maintain eye contact while turning the pages of your notes or manuscript. Avoid being conspicuous when you turn the pages. Use small pages or cards, or slide the pages aside rather than turning them.

Facial Expressions

The number of emotions that can be communicated through facial expressions is amazing. This may be the most direct means for a congregation to "read" a speaker. As with all areas of delivery, facial expressions should suggest, enforce, and support content. A smile should never be used, for example, when a frown is appropriate. The opposite is also true. Imagine a speaker forcefully speaking about the need for an attitude of love while glaring at the congregation! Or a preacher commenting on Paul's emphasis on joy in the Book of Philippians with a sad or expressionless look.

The chief problem most speakers have with facial expressions is that they have no idea what a facial expression looks like to a congregation. Most speakers justifiably want to avoid an appearance of superficiality, or of being overly dramatic. The result is that they are blind in the area of facial expression. Because the speaker needs to see what the congregation sees, a videotape is an invaluable aid. It enables the speaker to see what the congregation saw at the moment of delivery. Usually the speaker will recall feeling intense emotion, and is surprised that these emotions were not reflected in facial expression.

There is often a gap between what you as the speaker feel and what you actually communicate.

The best exercise for closing the gap between feeling and expression is to exaggerate various facial expressions. For instance, try smiling, and look in a mirror while holding the smile. If you see little if any smile in the mirror, broaden your smile. You may feel that the smile is too broad, but you may see in the mirror the smile you only felt was there before. This exercise helps the speaker coordinate what feels like a good smile with the amount of muscular activity required to produce that smile.

The best facial expressions occur when the speaker is rid of restricting inhibitions or cultural conditionings. The best facial expressions unconsciously reflect the emotions and feelings of a speaker.

Posture

The guidelines for good posture are more flexible than the guidelines for any other area of public speaking. In all areas of communication, individual differences are as numerous as individual speakers, and this is especially true of posture. The speaker should determine the most comfortable way to stand while communicating a sense of self-confidence and eagerness. Good posture for speaking is neither rigid nor slack. It simply provides a comfortable position from which vocal and other bodily expressions may be communicated. Therefore, a posture should be chosen that assists the smooth movement of head, arms, and torso.

The position of the feet is intrinsic to comfortable posture. Again, the speaker must determine which angle and space between the feet is comfortable. Look for a position that will help you shift the body smoothly to the front, back, or either side. The body is usually shifted by changing the position of the feet. For instance, the speaker may move one foot forward and then put most of the body weight on that foot. This causes a slight leaning toward the congregation and communicates a sense of urgency. Conversely, putting most of the body weight on the back foot communicates a sense of rejection or with-drawal. The individual speaker should work through the message and determine beforehand the various postures to be used. As always, posture and its changes should support content.

One of the chief distractions in the use of body in speaking is an unconscious shifting of weight from one foot to the other. The congregation sees this shifting as a swaying motion. Body swaying is usually done rhythmically and is almost always the result of unchanneled nervous energy. When body sway is a problem, the speaker should correct it by placing one foot slightly forward and placing most of the body weight on it.

Gestures

Good gestures are impulsive, but they are well-timed and well-coordinated actions of the entire body. To simplify discussion, we will discuss gestures only as they relate to the hands and arms.

Few of us talk without using our hands and arms. Speakers who do not use gestures have usually been carefully taught to resist the natural impulse to do so. Gestures can be a valuable asset to the speaker if they are spontaneously used in a way that supports content. Using your hands when speaking is not necessarily an undignified way to communicate. A man was observed by his wife describing a key play from the previous night's basketball game. The man was animated in expression and his listener was tantalized by the description. The speaker's wife interrupted him in midsentence with the question, "Can't you speak without using your hands?" The speaker paused with hands and arms frozen in midair in the gesture he was using before the interruption. With hands and arms still in the same position, he turned to his wife with a quizzical expression on his face and asked her, "Why would you want to?" Gestures should be impulsive reflections of the speaker's feelings. When they are, they will support and assist language and vocal expression.

Gestures must be timed to mesh with language and vocal

expression. Timing is especially important when a point is being emphasized. It would be ludicrous to make a vocal emphasis and then pound the pulpit two seconds later! Gestures must be timed to support content.

Gestures must be coordinated smoothly with other communicative actions. If an emphatic statement is to be made, facial expressions should reflect concern, posture should communicate urgency, and gestures should be emphatic. The body should work as a well-coordinated unit.

For most speakers, the major problem in the use of gestures is a feeling of self-consciousness. If we think about how to use our hands, we become conscious of them and this leads to inhibitions. That is the reason the best gestures are impulsive rather than planned. If a speaker is having difficulty obeying the impulse to use gestures, a few simple exercises will help.

1. The inhibited communicator will tend to "pin" his elbows to the sides of the body. Inadequate, half-arm gestures are the result. To break this habit, stand in an open area. Move the right arm across the body, with the arm nearly parallel to the floor. Next, in a slow, sweeping motion, move the arm until it is extended all the way to the right. Note that the elbow was not pinned to the side. Repeat the same exercise with the left arm. Now use both arms at the same time, just as a football referee would to signal an incomplete pass. These exercises will help you break the inhibition of moving your arms past the center line of your body. (This imaginary line is about the same vertical position as the spinal cord. Some speakers unconsciously develop an inhibition against moving their arms past that imaginary line.)

2. Another helpful exercise is to lift the hands, palms up, till the arms are just above a line parallel to the floor. Palms up indicates acceptance. To communicate rejection, stand with the elbows at the side and hands perpendicular to the floor. Now push the arms forward as if an object were being shoved out of the way. Finally, with the hands next to the shoulders and perpendicular to the floor, move them until the palms point down and the arms are parallel to the floor. This exercise

also communicates rejection. These exercises will help the speaker feel comfortable about using full-arm gestures.

Be careful that gestures do not become distracting. Too many of them may cause the listener to see only a flurry of motion. Rhythmic gestures will also draw attention away from the message. These are any repeated movements that appear to be in tune with some inaudible beat.

Vocal variables and body language should always support content. The vocal variables—rate, pitch, volume, and pause—support it by orally interpreting the ideas or concepts the speaker wishes to communicate. The vocal variables suggest emphases, telegraph transitions, give descriptions, communicate moods, and set the stage for congregational response. Body language supports content by reinforcing the vocal variables or, at times, by communicating a message that is not or cannot be communicated orally. Vocal variables and body language work spontaneously and harmoniously in support of content. They should not sound or look "staged," and their use should be synchronized.

Hercules Collins, an eighteenth-century English pastor, concluded a section of his chapter on "Ministerial Gifts" with sage advice on the deportment of the minister and management of voice:

> Let your Carriage and Habit in a Pulpit be grave and sober, let us have no indecent Behaviour, no uncomely Garb. . . . we must speak so loud as our Auditory may hear us, or else both the End of Preaching and Hearing is lost. And to be uneven in our Voice, to be sometimes very high and loud, and then presently very low, the former part of the Sentence may possibly be heard by most of all, but the latter part may not be heard by a sixth part of the People; so that they had almost as good heard nothing, if they cannot hear the whole Sentence. How is the End either of preaching or hearing answered in this? Isa. 58:1 Lift up thy Voice like a Trumpet. . . . And take heed of an affected Tone in preaching; let your Voice be natural, or else sound Doctrine may be liable to Contempt.[8]

8. Hercules Collins, *The Temple Repair'd* (London: William and Joseph Marshall, 1702), pp. 29-30.

Bible reading offers the widest scope for the enrichment of public worship and it is a great pity that the Scriptures are often so badly read.

When the Book is well read and made to live for the people, it can do for them what sermons often fail to do: it can be the very voice of God to their souls.

W. E. Sangster
The Approach to Preaching

5 Improving Oral Interpretation

"How do I put it all together?"

Full vocal production, clear enunciation, and the effective use of vocal variables and body language are all intrinsically related. We have treated them separately only for purposes of analysis. The speech discipline that integrates all the others is oral interpretation.

Oral interpretation is both a science and an art. It is a science because it requires hypothesis, analysis, experimentation, and a tentative conclusion. It is an art because the application of its conclusions calls for the physical and vocal expressions of various shades of meaning and feeling. *The scientific process* involves an analysis of the literature or concepts to be communicated. The nature and purpose of the information to be communicated must be determined by linguistic, lexical, historical, and psychological hypotheses, analysis, experiments, and tentative conclusions. The conclusions are tentative because the analysis rarely reaches a stage of final conclusion. *The artistic process* involves the subtle shading of physical and vocal expressions. These expressions depend on the integration of full vocal production, clear enunciation, and versatile use of the vocal variables and body language. Oral interpretation is the process that "puts together" the varied speech functions for effective communication.

A good technical definition of oral interpretation describes it as "the process by which a *reader,* communicating from a manuscript through vocal and physical *suggestions,* stimulates a listener response that is favorable to the reader's judgments of the intent of the literature."[1]

Oral interpretation, then, involves *literature,* a *reader* who suggests the meaning of the literature, and *listeners* who follow the suggestions of the reader. We will expand this definition as we apply it to public speaking. The term *literature* will include not only material written by someone else (e.g., the Bible), but it will also include manuscripts, notes, or extemporaneous messages prepared by the person designated as the reader. "Reader" will be expanded to include not only the person who reads a portion of Scripture or other literature, but also the person who publicly speaks a message (e.g., a sermon, or a devotional thought). We do not need to expand the definition of "listeners."

A key word for understanding the oral interpreter's task is "suggestion." Suggestion falls short of dramatizing the message being presented, but moves well beyond the mere utterance of words. The oral interpreter attempts to suggest the meaning, the ethos (the emotional qualities) of the message in a way that brings the listeners to an identical or similar level of understanding. If the oral interpreter wishes to suggest an attitude of *agape* (the Greek word for self-sacrificing love), then physical and vocal expressions that suggest that kind of love must be used. "The oral interpreter *works with* the listener rather than *performing for* the listener. The oral interpreter *suggests,* and if his focal and physical expressions are vivid and

1. Keith Brooks, Eugene Bahn, LaMont Okey, *The Communicative Act of Oral Interpretation* (Boston: Allyn & Bacon, 1975), pp. 25-26. Italics mine.

accurate, the listener will be able to *fulfill* those suggestions in his own mind."[2]

Dramatizing calls for extreme involvement by the speaker. If one were reading from Matthew 5, for example, you would speak as loudly in an enclosed auditorium as Jesus did on the mount in the open air. If you were describing the emotional agony of King David, you would fall to the floor or lift your hands to heaven or stamp your feet and cry, "Absalom, Absalom, O my son Absalom . . ." in the way you assume David did. Dramatization serves a special purpose in a dramatic monologue or in theater presentation; however, suggestion is much more suitable to a worship service.

Merely speaking words may be less satisfactory than dramatization. When the vocal variables are used in a narrow range or monotone, and the body language is placid, the speaker communicates a disdain for the message, whether one reads it or speaks it extemporaneously. Again, suggestion is far superior.

Unlimited variations occur in individual speaker styles and abilities. Therefore, no specific warning signals can be given to advise when a speaker has gone beyond oral interpretation to dramatization (or, for that matter, when the speaker has arrived at suggestion from the lower level of mere utterances of words). But some general guidelines can help the speaker become more effective in reading and speaking. Some of these guidelines presume a working knowledge of full vocal production, clear enunciation, effective use of the vocal variables and body language, and the ability to use language in a clear manner. Our general hypothesis is this: good oral interpretation "puts together" speech and linguistic skills in a way that maximizes the message and minimizes the messenger.

Public Reading

Analysis Stage

1. Determine beforehand the nature of the literature to be read. Read the passage aloud several times and concentrate on

2. Brooks, Bahn, Okey, *Communicative Act,* p. 26.

its meaning. While reading, ask yourself: What type of literature is this? Is it poetry, such as Psalm 23? Is it history, such as Joshua 24? Is it public oration, such as the Sermon on the Mount? Who is speaking? Who is listening? (As an example, understanding Jesus' audience helps the interpretation of Luke 15.) Why are they listening? What is the setting—temple worship? Private conversation? Questions such as these will lead to an understanding of the meaning or purpose of the passage.

2. Distinguish the supporting ideas from the main idea of the passage. The author will usually explain, expand, or amplify the main idea. The speaker should not overemphasize these supporting ideas, unless there is some specific purpose for doing so. For instance, the phrase ". . . he humbled Himself . . ." in Philippians 2:8 supports the imperative, "Let this mind be in you, which was also in Christ Jesus . . ." in Philippians 2:5. Verse five, then, should receive more emphatic suggestion than verse seven. (If a speaker wishes to emphasize verse seven for some reason, it is advisable first to read the entire passage with accurate oral interpretation. Then return to verse seven, mentioning that it will be a focal passage even though it is one of the supporting ideas to the main idea in verse five.)

3. Determine the proper word groupings. The grouping of words between pauses in speech is known as phrasing. Punctuation marks are important, but they may not always be the final determinants for oral phrasing. Read a passage aloud and vary the phrasings. Notice how changes in phrasing change the meaning of this passage (the slash marks represent pauses):

> And I / said the Lord / must be high and lifted up.
> And I said / the Lord must be high and lifted up.
> And I said the Lord must be high and lifted up.

The first phrase indicates that the Lord is the source of the quote. The second phrase indicates that the speaker is the source of the quote. The third phrase, spoken without a pause, indicates that the speaker is the source of the quote, and suggests that the quote is not important.

Experimental Stage

4. Determine which words and phrases should be emphasized. Vocal emphasis is achieved in the following ways: (1) by
inflecting pitch a little higher on a specific phrase, word, or
syllable. Without changing volume, say the following question
aloud with higher inflection on the fourth word: "Is that story
really true?" Try a passage of Scripture, this time emphasizing
the personal pronoun by using inflection, "Sir, what must I do
to be saved?" Try a conversational phrase, again keeping the
volume level but inflecting every word: "Hi, son, Get in, let's
go." Say the same words again, this time using no inflection.
The first greeting sounded cheerful because of inflections;
however, the second greeting sounded solemn because of a
lack of inflection. By alternating the placing of the emphasis, a
"feel" for the meaning of the passage can be established. Try
this slight paraphrase of John 2:5, emphasizing only the capital-
ized words:

"AND Mary said / whatsoever He says to do / you do it."

The emphasis on the conjunction *and* is obviously misplaced.
Read the passage aloud again, this time emphasizing the next
word:

"and MARY said / whatsoever He says to do / you do it."

The emphasis on "Mary" is not necessary here, since she has
already been identified in the preceding verses. We will skip
the word *said* in the exercise and try the emphasis on the next
word:

"and Mary said / WHATSOEVER He says to do / you do it."

This reading makes much more sense than the first two. Continue this exercise through the end of the sentence. Notice
that each time the emphasis is changed, the meaning is altered.

In speaking, make certain to place the emphasis on the correct words and phrases.

The degree of emphasis can be varied. Some passages may have no words or phrases that need major emphasis. Other passages may have words and phrases that call for varying degrees of major and minor emphasis. In still other passages, only one word should receive the emphasis. These should be determined before you walk to the platform.

5. Look for transitions and contrasts. Transitions accomplish several purposes: they provide movement from one subject to another, from one idea to another, or from one emotion to another. They may also be used to indicate any number of changes in setting or character. A transition may be as brief as a single word: *moreover, therefore,* or *however.* The words *well* and *now* are words for transition, and are grossly overused by preachers. Transitions may also be phrases, such as, "on the other hand." Or transitions may be complete sentences: "We have seen that Jesus is divine. Next, we will see that Jesus is also human." Transitions are expressed by a combination of inflection, pause, and body language, as dictated by content. For example: "The voice may convey a transition by a change from a fuller to a lighter tone, or from a quick tempo to a slower tempo, or the reverse. It may change from a major key to a sad, melancholy key or from a staccato to legato movement. You may indicate a transition by a slight shift of the body, a change of posture, or a movement of the head."[3]

Contrasts obviously involve the presentation of opposites. The use of contrasts can deepen the emotional experience, as when Jesus said, "you have heard it said, 'An eye for an eye, and a tooth for a tooth,' but I say unto you. . . ." Contrasts can best be expressed by variations in pitch level, pitch inflection, volume, and rate. Experiment with these word variables and, as always, strive for oral interpretation that supports content.

Tentative Conclusion Stage

6. The final step in adapting oral interpretation to speaking is to bring all of the preceding steps together—hypothesis,

---

3. Brooks, Bahn, Okey, *Communicative Act,* p. 155.

analysis, experiment, and tentative conclusion. The reader should use full vocal production, clear enunciation, vocal variables, and body language to communicate the final determination of the meaning of the passage. We know that John 2:5 narrates a conversation between Mary, Jesus, and two or more unnamed servants at a wedding feast in someone's home (*hypothesis*). Apparently Mary is speaking in the imperative, because Jesus has thus far resisted her suggestions. John refers to this incident as the first miracle of Jesus (*analysis*). We can conclude from this that John did not record the event to prove that Mary exerted matriarchal authority. This event is recorded so that we may know the first miracle of Jesus. By logical extension, then, we can presume that this passage deals with the lordship of Jesus. The details of the miracle, the changing of water into wine, we can deduce, are secondary to the fact that Jesus gave evidence of His lordship in many ways, one of which was the performing of miracles.

With these facts in mind, we can *experiment*. First, say aloud "and Mary said" without emphasis. Next, speak the quote evenly, but with some emphasis: "Whatsoever He says to do/you do it!" Next, let's experiment with some varying degrees of emphasis: "Whatsoever He says to do / YOU DO IT." The best oral interpretation probably lies somewhere between these two examples. The reader is responsible for developing the artistic use of vocal and physical expression that will convey the reader's suggested interpretation to the listeners (*tentative conclusion*). The speaker's ability in this area will grow with experience.

The authors of *Basic Principles of Speech* summarized the task as follows: "Writing, like notes in music, is just black marks on paper. But, like notes in music, it represents ideas, feelings, meanings that *lived* in the mind of the author or composer. The oral reader's job is to bring those black marks back to life in his own mind and body. Then, much as the violinist turns a musical score back into music, the reader uses his own mind, voice, and body as the instrument for making language come back to life for his listeners."[4]

4. Sarrett, Foster, Sarrett, *Basic Principles*, p. 142.

This should be especially true in the public reading of Scripture. It is amazing how many preachers staunchly defend the Bible, but read it aloud as if they had rarely seen it. Many preachers have the congregation stand "in respect for the reading of God's Holy Word." Standing may be one way to demonstrate respect for God's Word. But standing or sitting, the congregation should never hear Scripture read atrociously, monotonously, offhandedly, or laboriously, as if it were a task to be endured before the performance of the speaker. *The public reading of Scripture should be a highlight in the worship service.* Good oral interpretation will magnify the Word of God without calling attention to itself. A preacher or any reader of the Bible should be satisfied with no less than an inspiring, uplifting reading that can become ". . . the very voice of God to their souls."

Public Proclamation

The proclaimer's task at this point is more simple than that of the reader. The first three steps for the reader are not necessary for the proclaimer, since the proclaimer has prepared the message (literature) that is to be communicated to the listeners. The proclaimer may be speaking from a manuscript, notes, or extemporaneously. Whatever the case, he must now incorporate reader's guidelines four, five, and six (see above) with only minor adjustments. The guidelines for the proclaimer are as follows:

1. Practice the message aloud. Experiment with the vocal variables and body language until you find the best way to suggest the purpose or meaning of the message. Be careful not to be loud just for the sake of being loud. Save the major emphases for those portions of the message that require it. Vary the rate so that relatively unimportant sections move a little more quickly than major assertions and conclusions. (Explanations and applications usually are spoken more slowly than illustrations.) Use pitch inflections to indicate transitions and to assist in making emphases. Use pauses to give the

listener time to absorb information, or to set the stage for a major emphasis.

The first sentence of a sermon, for instance, should always be spoken conversationally, unless there's some reason to shout it or whisper it. The first sentence may be the mundane, "The text for today is. . . ." It may also immediately involve the congregation in some way: "You will recall that it was in 1973 that American prisoners of war were finally released from North Vietnam." It would be ludicrous to shout or whisper either of these opening sentences. In both cases, content calls for a conversational tone. The proclaimer should always let content dictate how the message will be orally interpreted to the listeners.

2. Use a tape recorder (video, if possible) to evaluate the delivery of recent messages and to improve the delivery of future messages. Again, the best technique for evaluation and self-improvement is to transcribe a message (or portion of it) from the tape recorder just as it was preached. Remember, you will experience an initial shock when you see in writing what you said. A strong side benefit of transcribing messages is that the intellectual message will be presented more clearly in future speaking opportunities.

A video transcription lets the speaker see and hear the message. This permits an analysis of both the "literature" and the delivery. Listen carefully to see if important sections were communicated with emphasis, and if relatively unimportant sections were de-emphasized. Watch for inflections and pauses that communicate transition from one thought to another. Listen for monotones, vocal patterns, and distracting habits such as lip smacking, vocalized pauses, or lazy speech. If you have a video tape, look to see if eye contact was strong, especially during key assertions. See if the body language supported and helped communicate the content. Watch for any distracting mannerisms such as body sway, rhythmic gestures, and annoying habits such as constantly pushing glasses up on the nose or licking the lips. These evaluation sessions will gradually dissolve hindrances to good speaking and enhance communication techniques that are effective.

These evaluation sessions should take place only before and after speaking opportunities—never during. If they are done during a presentation, the speaker will be preoccupied in a way that will hinder the delivery, and the attention of the audience will be removed from the message. All of us make minor adjustments as we speak, but thorough evaluations should not take place during the proclamation.

The various speech techniques are not designed to call attention to themselves. If a congregation admires a speaker's voice or speech techniques, or it holds the communication process itself above the message being proclaimed, then the speaker has failed. The speech techniques in this book lead ideally to *image-level communication.* That is, the listeners are led to "see" in their minds what the speaker is saying. Each word, phrase, sentence, and paragraph should be so supportive of content that the congregation can literally picture what is being said. (Abstract ideas should be made concrete for the congregation.) Image-level communication means that the congregation will be looking at the speaker, who is an acceptable and credible source of information to them, but they will be seeing the speaker only through the message being proclaimed. (Many preachers pray, "Lord, hide me behind thy cross as I preach!" This book is an attempt to put hands, feet, body, and voice into that prayer.)

Image-level communication allows the congregation not only to "see" that which is being said, but it also lets them "feel" it. When this kind of empathy is established, the listener is much more likely to respond to the speaker's invitation to take some specific action or to change an attitude. With image-level communication, commitments and attitude changes are much more likely to be permanent than if the speaker depends on such devices as speech techniques, special gimmicks, or personal charm.

Careful preparation is necessary to maximize the message and minimize the messenger. Full vocal production gives the speaker the means of realizing the full potential of individual voice quality, and at the same time it preserves and protects the voice for service in the later years of life. Clear enunciation puts a congregation at ease for they can listen to the message without trying to figure out what the speaker has said. Vocal variables give meaning to the language. Body language reinforces the language, and at times it even serves in place of language. Oral interpretation integrates all of these speech functions in a way that makes language come alive for the listener.

In preaching, as in most forms of Christian oral communication, we must remember that delivery is subservient to content. Both the message and the messenger are vital to preaching. Take one or the other away, and preaching cannot exist. But sermon content is always more important than sermon delivery. The messenger is never more important than the message being proclaimed. Then why a book on sermon delivery? Because ineffective delivery focuses attention on itself. Effective delivery, however, points beyond itself by supporting the message we have been commissioned to proclaim.

*We take radio and television for granted now, but (in
1926) radio was new, and its use for religious purposes
was in an experimental stage. . . . I had no idea of the pos-
sibilities involved. Frankly skeptical of its effect, I under-
took it rather listlessly. I used to go down to the studio on
Sunday afternoons and, sitting at a table, talk into that
strange contrivance, the microphone, with no vivid sense
of contact with the unseen audience. Later the microphone became to me almost as stirring as a great congregation, no longer a thing, but an almost living symbol of
multitudes of individual people. . . .*

Harry Emerson Fosdick
The Living of These Days

6 Delivery for Radio and Television

"How do I preach on radio and television?"

Broadcast historians have varying opinions about
when the first radio "program" was transmitted. For convenience in documentation, most of them recognize the coverage
of the presidential election returns of 1920 on KDKA in Pitts-
burgh, Pennsylvania, as the first radio broadcast. Probably it
was the first program aired by a commercial radio station.
Several broadcasts were made by radio experimenters prior to
1920.

A Canadian experimenter named Reginald Aubrey Fessenden
broadcast a radio "program" to ships at sea on Christmas Eve,
1906.[1] This may have been the first attempt to broadcast for

1. A. F. Harlow, *Old Wires and New Waves* (New York: Appleton-Century, 1936),
p. 455.

other than experimental purposes. Imagine the astonishment of the radio operators who were accustomed to hearing only dots and dashes blipped into their headphones, when they suddenly heard a voice! This first program was Christian. Fessenden read Luke 2:1-20; a female vocalist sang a piece from Handel's *Messiah;* a poem was read; and then a violin solo of "O Holy Night" was played. The broadcast concluded with a brief speech that was probably a sermon or devotional thought.

In the 1920s, sixty-three churches were licensed to operate radio stations. The economic depression of the 1930s forced most churches to sell their stations. Most commercial stations of that decade were network affiliated. The networks, especially NBC, provided religious and other public service programming and required their affiliate stations carry them free of charge. This forced local stations to charge the churches for air time. This policy of assessing a fee for broadcast time for local churches still exists. It was firmly adopted by local television stations as soon as they were established.

Requiring churches to pay for air time has an additional advantage to providing revenue. It is one way that local radio and television stations can screen applicants for broadcast times. The local station is responsible for both the technical quality and the content of any program it puts on the air. Some stations have been embarrassed by both poor quality and poor content in religious programs. For that reason, local church leaders (or anyone wishing to purchase air time for a religious program) are often required to convince the station manager or program director that they are dependable, responsible persons of integrity. One way for the church or person who requests air time to accomplish this is for them to ask to be familiarized with broadcast law and with the station's technical equipment. Local station managers will appreciate this interest in helping them both obey broadcast laws and produce programs of acceptable technical quality.

Speaking on radio or television is only slightly different from speaking to a local congregation. In fact, much religious programming is the broadcast of a local Sunday morning worship service. Some guidelines, however, should be followed to guarantee a successful operation.

Guidelines for Christian Programs on Radio

1. The radio audience will picture the speaker in their minds. Their mental image rarely stands the test of reality. With few exceptions, when a listener meets the speaker, he will generally say, "You do not look at all like you sound." The speaker cannot control these mental images of physical appearance, but can do much by way of conveying a mental impression of the speaker as a person. "Even without the assistance of visual cues, it is clear that a listener is responding not only to message content but to the "image of the speaker."[2] Holtzman adds: ". . . the listeners are not necessarily responding to the speaker as he actually exists. They are responding to the *perceived* speaker as he is comprehended and interpreted by the listeners' nervous systems."[3] *The goal should be to speak in a manner that is authoritative, urgent, and sincere. Authoritative*—meaning that the message is based on the Bible. *Urgent*—meaning that the speaker has a message the listener needs. *Sincere*—meaning that the speaker does not share the message for personal gain, but because the listeners need to hear it for their own good. The listeners should feel that if the speaker were available, it would be nice to invite him or her over for dinner. That kind of confidence is necessary if the listener is to receive the speaker as a credible source.

2. Of necessity, broadcasters are slaves to the clock. The station manager or program director usually will state some time limits for a local program. The perils of ignoring time limits in any broadcast operation are obvious. If a local church, for example, buys an hour of air time per week for 10:00 A.M.

2. John H. Court, "Paralinguistic Cues in Religious Broadcasting," *Journal of Psychological Theology* (Winter, 1978), p. 40.

3. P. D. Holtzman, *The Psychology of Speaker's Audiences* (Glenview: Scott, Foresman, and Co., 1970), p. 7.

Sunday, and another church is scheduled for 11:00 A.M., the time limit *must be closely observed.* If the ten o'clock program lasts 60 minutes/15 seconds, the eleven o'clock church program will either be put on the air late or will be joined in progress. Either way, listeners generally will conclude, "Our local station messed up again." If the ten o'clock program lasts fifty-six minutes instead of fifty-nine minutes, the local station must either play organ music and/or read public service announcements until the three minute time gap is filled.

3. Be sure that the *technical quality* of your program is acceptable. This is usually a problem for the church that has its own recording equipment. (Churches that record or broadcast their programs on station equipment usually will not have this concern.) Reliable and efficient broadcast equipment is not cheap, and it must be maintained.

A local church considering the purchase of its own equipment would be wise to consult technicians in the field. It would also be wise to make budget provisions for both the *initial purchase* of its equipment and for its *continued maintenance.*

4. Be certain that the *content* of the program does not cause unnecessary difficulty for the local radio station. A conference with the station manager will clarify current Federal Communications Commission laws pertaining to the fairness doctrine. This doctrine demands that licensed stations devote time to controversial issues, but that they always afford equal time for opposing viewpoints. The fairness doctrine laws came into being in 1929.[4] As with many legal matters, challenges to this law have caused constant adjustments and crystalization. The local station justifies its existence by serving the public interest, convenience, or necessity of the local community. Religious programming is considered to be in the public interest and convenience, but it is subject to the fairness doctrine. The

4. For an interesting account of the history of the fairness doctrine, see Fred Friendly, *The Good Guys and the Bad Guys: Free Speech vs. Fairness in Broadcasting* (New York: Random House, 1975).

church-related programs should be completely devoted to preaching the gospel. But when the gospel message or subject matter of the program involves controversial issues, such as abortion, race relations, or homosexuality, the local broadcaster is bound by law to give persons with opposing viewpoints the opportunity to express their side of the issue.

Ideally, the content of the radio program should be basic information that meets some vital need.[5] Rare and perhaps nonexistent is the radio audience, for example, that is prepared to listen to a discussion about the history of the Kenites. The speaker who has trouble with this point would do well to purchase a red-letter edition of the New Testament and study the simple, profound words of Jesus. The radio message should focus on some vital concern of the audience, such as problems in the contemporary home.

Human interest is also a vital ingredient to a good content on a radio program. To create human interest, simply mention people as you prepare the content. The biblical text of the message usually will involve one or more persons. Again, we can learn from Jesus: "A certain man had two sons. . . ." "A sower went out to sow. . . ." Including people in the message has many additional biblical precedents. The Bible, to borrow a fitting rural phrase, is "chock full" of people. Every doctrine in the Bible relates itself to people. Acts 17:16-34, for instance, loses its impact if it is studied only as a lesson in audience psychology. Paul and the varied reactions of his congregation are vital to the life of the story. Why, the Bible begins with the Person who created humanity. Modern preachers can learn much from it about the importance of the human element in communication. Human interest prohibits a dry, abstract message that lacks image-level communication.

Word pictures are also vital to the content of a radio program. These pictures need not be elaborate, but they should be

<hr>

5. For a brief discussion of preaching that is basic and vital see Raymond Bailey, "Vital Preaching," *The Baptist Program* (Nov. 1974), p. 4; and Richard G. Watson, "What's Wrong with Preaching Today?" *Christianity Today*, (Oct. 25, 1975), p. 27.

specific. Think, for example, of how many synonyms are available for the verb *walk,* and how each one conveys a different picture.

The lady walked into the store. (Image-level communication is weak.)

The lady shuffled into the store. (a specific picture!)

The lady strutted into the store. (an entirely different picture!)

A thesaurus is invaluable to the radio speaker in developing a vocabulary that will improve image level communication.

Avoid the use of preaching clichés that take several forms. The following examples were taken from various sermons the author has heard.

Preacher Talk

"Turn over in your Bibles . . ." (someone may take that literally).

"Turn with me, if you would . . ." ("if you would" may be courteous, but it is overworked).

"Beloved" or "brethren" (never used in conversation except by preachers).

Hyperbolic Hyperbole

"This is the most tragic story you will ever hear . . ." (until next Sunday, when I must come up with another tear-jerker).

"The temple was completely destroyed, completely demolished, completely ravaged, completely ruined . . ." (and every redundancy ruins the impact of the word preceding it).

Doublespeak[6]

". . . a few short miles to church . . ." (are these miles less than 5,280 feet?).

". . . a few brief minutes . . ." (again, do some minutes contain less than sixty seconds?)

---

6. D. G. Kehl used this word in his incisive article, "Have You Committed Verbicide Today?" *Christianity Today,* (January 28, 1978), pp. 18-21.

Overstating the Obvious

"The President was assassinated two days ago. As he was being driven through a downtown street, waving to the cheering crowd, shots rang out. . . ." (Who in the congregation would not know the details two days later?).

Technical Jargon

"Are you responding to the promise of the coming eschaton?" (This question was asked of a *new* convert!)

Abuse of Technical Language

"Obviously Peter is using an anacoluthon . . ." (impressive sounding, but way above the heads of the congregation).

Misleading Word Order

"With a broken tail bone and a fractured skull, I shall never forget . . ." (no, the preacher meant someone else had a broken tail bone and fractured skull, not himself).

"Preacher talk" conveys the image of a "professional religionist," not that of a warm person who has an urgent and vital message.

Guidelines for Christian Programs on Television

Television broadcasting has much more impact and prestige connected with it than radio broadcasting. This is because of the number of hours spent watching television by society as a whole, and because the audience can make a visual as well as audio evaluation of the speaker. The number of hours per week per household spent watching television varies from a general low of about twenty to a general high of around thirty. The effect of that amount of television viewing on the individual and collective psyche has yet to be measured. In fact, we are only now learning which questions to ask in measuring the influence of television on the way a person thinks. The opening salvoes in this field of study have only recently been fired.

John R. W. Stott sees at least five negative influences: (1) physical laziness, (2) intellectual passiveness, (3) emotional insensitivity, (4) psychological confusion, and (5) moral disorder.[7]

Stott asks: ". . . how easily can people switch from one world (television) to the other? Do they recognize, when they hear God's word and worship him, that now at least they are in touch with eternal reality? Or do they, as I fear, move from one unreal situation to another, somnambulating as in a dream, because television has introduced them to a world of fantasy from which they never escape?"[8]

The moral question has also been raised by Martin E. Marty:

> The media . . . set out to shape in men "the proper opinions," to make them common men and women, unknown citizens somehow at the mercy of the communicator. Because of the hours of attention they command and the apparent quality that is theirs owing to the economic potential, they usually achieve this aim. It is in such a world that Christianity makes its claim and its offer. It presents a paradox, a foolishness, something "contrary to the opinion." It has an improper opinion for the uncommon man; for the known citizen of the commonwealth whose builder and maker is God.[9]

Harold J. Ellens quoted this excerpt from Marty's book and expressed the same concern: "The mass media has become potent arbiters of value in our society, and the cultural and spiritual idealism they communicate will eventually shape our culture and society. In the final analysis, humans become in large part what they are taught to digest and/or confess."[10]

The local church or individual Christian who aspires to

7. John R. W. Stott, *Between Two Worlds: The Art of Preaching in the 20th Century* (Grand Rapids: Eerdmans, 1982), pp. 70-73.

8. Ibid., p. 73.

9. Martin E. Marty, *The Improper Opinion* (Philadelphia: Westminster Press, 1961), p. 32.

10. Harold J. Ellens, *Models of Religious Broadcasting* (Grand Rapids: Eerdmans, 1974), p. 147.

communicate a Christian message on television must be aware of the ethical as well as technical problems in program production. The Christian broadcaster, then, must concentrate on presenting a positive gospel message that relates to the needs and hurts of the contemporary audience.

The Christian broadcaster should ardently avoid building a cult of personality. This is a great temptation for many persons who appear on television. The effect seems to be, ". . . if you really matter, you will be at the focus of mass attention, and if you are at the focus of mass attention, then surely you must really matter."[11] The use of television increases the temptation to promote the messenger rather than the message. That is hardly a new phenomenon. Acts 19:13-16 records how two men tried to exploit the name of Jesus and paid an embarrassing price for their efforts! It behooves all Christian workers, especially those in broadcasting, to read carefully Acts 12:22-24 and Acts 14:11-15. In Christian broadcasting, therefore, the imperative to magnify the message and minimize the messenger is critically important.

The technical suggestions for producing a Christian television program are based on some of those outlined for radio: (1) remember that the station is a slave to the clock, (2) use the facilities of a local television station or be certain that your program is recorded on high-quality equipment that is regularly maintained, and (3) be certain that the content is appealing and does not cause unnecessary difficulty for the local station. Several considerations should be added, however.

1. Remember that television is a visual medium. This seems obvious enough, but many persons treat television merely as an audio medium in which the audience sees the speaker. The most boring picture on television is the "talking head." (A talking head is a picture of the speaker looking at the camera with the lens zoomed in so that the viewer sees only the

11. Paul S. Lazarsfeld and Robert K. Merton, "Mass Communication, Popular Taste, and Organized Social Action," in *The Process and Effects of Mass Communication,* ed. Wilburn Schramm and Donald E. Roberts (Chicago: University of Illinois Press, 1972), pp. 561-562.

shoulders, neck, and head of the speaker.) Plan to give variety by using slides, movies, and photographs that picture the content of the message. Observe how various programs and commercials use not only the actors, but other visual stimuli. Notice how briefly each picture or camera angle is on the screen before it is changed. This "flitting" of pictures may not be good for the Christian program because it limits attention span. These production decisions need to be thought through and evaluated by the local church if it is to make maximum use of television as a visual medium.

2. Be aware of on-camera stage presence. Stage presence communicates either a sense of rapport and self-confidence or a lack of it. Notice the contrasts in a program that calls for members of the audience to appear on stage. The host always seems to look "just right," but the audience participant conveys a sense of awkwardness. Because the host has many years of experience, he will act with authority. (Most of us develop a sense of relaxation, self-confidence, and authority as we gain experience in any endeavor. This is especially true in broadcasting.)

The difference will also be noted in the use of body language. The professional will stand or sit at a slight angle to the camera more often than facing the camera directly. The slight angle conveys a sense of relaxed conversation. With notable exceptions, however, facing the camera directly tends to convey a sense of confrontation. Notice also that the professional uses good posture (neither rigid nor slouched). The professional will have a low eye-blink rate (the frequency of eye blinking conveys a feeling of insecurity). The professional does not use numerous gestures, unless they are necessary. The general physical appearance of the professional appears to be good, usually full of vitality and trim in appearance.

The amateur in broadcasting can acquire these professional qualities. Chapters two through five of this book are basic to achieving the "professional" look on television. The exception is this: gestures must be slow and deliberate on television, and they must never be made directly toward the camera. To put these techniques into practice and achieve good on-camera stage presence, the amateur will need to fight the following negative tendencies:

(1) Do not be disappointed if the local television station does not have a chapel from which religion programs are telecast. The set for a program is never so attractive as it appears on screen. The "chapel" will be made of cardboard backdrops located in a corner of a massive studio, and the bare concrete floor will be covered with heavy electrical wires. A forest of lights will droop from the ceiling, and they will be bright and warm. The speaker will want to become acclimated to the brightness slowly because the heat from the bulbs will eventually wilt the appearance of the speaker.

(2) When the floor director calls for you to take your place on the set, do not be intimidated by the situation. Look upon this moment as an opportunity to speak to people about Christ. The floor director will position the speaker at a slight angle to the camera. The speaker should keep the head high and place the body weight on the front foot. To do so will avoid a sense of withdrawal and intimidation. As noted before, the audience will be more attracted to a clear message from a person who communicates a sense of urgency and sincerity rather than one who creates a sense of uncertainty and timidity.

(3) Maintain strong eye contact with the camera. Even when visuals are used, the speaker should not be caught on camera reading from notes or a manuscript.

(4) Avoid looking at the monitor while on camera. The monitor will help you know when supplementary visuals are on the screen. Do not glance at the monitor to see how you "look" on television.

(5) Advise people who come along not to ask the director if they can be seen on camera sometime during the program. This is often true of choir members who are afraid they will be lost in a sea of faces. Television production crew personnel say that these requests, which are numerous, generally begin this way: "Sir, I would not ask this for myself, but I have a sick grandmother and it would make her feel ever so good if you would direct the camera on me during the choir number. You

understand it doesn't make any difference to me. . . ." The production crew often wonders whether anyone does a Christian program only for the glory of God.

3. Maintain a vivacious, energetic level throughout the program. Leave the audience feeling that you have more to say and plenty of energy to say it, but that you simply ran out of time. This will give the audience a feeling of looking forward to the next program. The speaker who ends the program with a gravelly voice, beleaguered expression, slouching posture, coat off, tie loose, top button of shirt unbuttoned, soaked with sweat, and standing on six inches of his trousers legs leaves the audience feeling that they have seen and heard all that this man has to offer, and that next week would merely be a repeat. (In fact, this is one of the dangers of cult of personality in religious programming. The audience should be looking forward to the message, not to the performance of the messenger.)

Good recent information has been published about the writing and production of television programs. The Christian broadcaster should be familiar with the technical aspects of telecasting. Television ethics should be of vital concern to the Christian broadcaster. Questions related to the influence of television on the way people perceive reality have been raised recently by Marshall McLuhan, Malcolm Muggeridge, J. Harold Ellens, Martin Marty, Everett C. Parker, and others. The Christian radio and television program should seek to attain the highest technical quality, appeal to a large audience, urgently share the message of Christ, and use the powerful influence of television in the best possible ways. Television should never be used for personal aggrandizement. This is especially true for the Christian broadcaster. The first television preacher to receive wide acclaim was Bishop Fulton J. Sheen. He avoided building a cult of personality by applying this strong biblical dictum:

On television, he who appears before the public may well ask himself: "What powers hast thou, that did not come to thee by gift? And if they came to thee by gift, why dost thou boast of them as if there were no gift in question? . . . No praise therefore is due the author of these telecasts. If there be gratitude for putting them into print, the author accepts it as the window receives light; namely, to pass thanks back again to God, the author of all good gifts. However, the imperfections, the failings, and the marring of the gifts are due to the window itself.[12]

Christians involved in radio and television programming should ardently avoid the temptation to build personal empires by magnifying their message and minimizing the messenger.

12. Fulton J. Sheen, *Life Is Worth Living* (Garden City, New York: Garden City Books, 1953), p. viii.

Appendix A
Self-evaluation for Voice Quality

1. Were my vocal bands sore before, during, or after the sermon?

2. Did I feel any vocal strain while preaching?

3. Do I hear any vocal strain in my preaching?

4. Was my optimum pitch level high during the sermon?

5. Was my breathing affected by tension before or during the sermon?

6. When I inhale, is it audible?

If any of the above questions are answered yes, practice the exercises in chapter two.

7. Plot a graph for an entire sermon, indicating when your voice was clear and strong and when it may have become strained, perhaps causing a retreat to dramatic whisper.

strong

about right
for me

weak

     introduction   body   conclusion   invitation

Appendix B
Self-evaluation for Clear Speech

1. List any misarticulated sounds in your sermon:
   1)
   2)
   3)
   4)
   5)
2. Were these misarticulated sounds caused by lazy speech habits?
3. Did rapid speech cause you to slur some words?

If the answer to any of these questions is yes, review chapter three. Give special attention to the specific sounds you did not articulate clearly in your sermon.

Appendix C
Self-evaluation for Vocal Variables

Pitch

1. Were my inflections clear and sharp enough to communicate transitions?

2. Were my inflections clear and sharp enough to communicate emphases?

3. Was my use of pitch restricted to a narrow range?

4. Do I detect any monotonous patterns in pitch?

If any of these questions are answered yes, turn to chapter four and review the information about pitch.

5. Plot a graph of your entire sermon showing *general* variations in pitch. If pitch is being used effectively, it will be difficult to plot this graph. If pitch is patterned or in a narrow range, the graph will be relatively simple to plot.

6. Plot a graph for a brief segment of your sermon, preferably where transitions and emphases occur. Beneath the graph, write the sentence in which the transitions or emphases appear. Study the relationship between pitch and content. Does pitch support content?

Volume

1. Is volume loud most of the time?
2. Is volume soft most of the time?
3. Is there a predictable pattern in volume levels?
4. Am I loud during less significant segments of my sermon?
5. Am I soft during more significant segments of my sermon?

If the answer to any of these questions is yes, review the information in chapter four about volume.

6. Plot a graph of the general volume level for your entire sermon. Again, this will be difficult if volume is used effectively, and relatively simple if volume is in a narrow range or a predictable pattern.

high

low

introduction   body   conclusion   invitation

7. Plot a graph for one of the key emphases of the sermon. If possible, write the words of this key segment beneath the graph and study the relationship between content and volume. Does volume support content?

high

low

"   "

8. Plot a similar graph for one of the less significant segments of
the sermon. Check to see if volume was emphatic or if it was at
a properly reduced level at this time.

high

low

"   "

Rate

1. Transcribe 60 seconds of your sermon from a tape. How many
words did you transcribe? More than 150? Less than 100? If you
count more than 150, determine if the content was relatively
less significant, and that a rapid rate was justified. If you count
less than 100, are you sure that content was that emphatic, and
that your deliberate approach was justified?
2. Transcribe the entire sermon, using vertical marks (|) to isolate
sixty-second segments. This will clearly outline where the rate
was fast or slow, and if the rate varied much at all.

250 wpm

200 wpm

150 wpm

100 wpm

50 wpm

        introduction   body   conclusion   invitation

Pause

1. Use the transcription made for study of rate. With a different color ink, put a slash mark (/) between words that received a pause. (Count only pauses of one second or more.) You may want to use different colors or varying sizes of slash marks to indicate longer or shorter pauses.
2. Review the transcript to see if any transitions or emphases did not receive a pause. (For instance, moving from the end of the reading of the text to the first word of the introduction.)

Gestures and Facial Expressions

1. Did gestures and facial expressions say the same thing as content? (Did I smile when I spoke of Job?)
2. Did gestures and facial expressions say the same thing as content? (They should not precede or come after content has been spoken.)
3. Did gestures and facial expressions cause distractions? (Too many of them?)
4. Do I use a particular gesture or facial expression too often?
5. Are my gestures rhythmic?
6. Do my gestures and facial expressions seem too dramatic?

Review the information and exercises in chapter four if questions 1 or 2 were answered no or if questions 3, 4, 5, or 6 were answered yes.

Appendix D
Self-evaluation for Oral Interpretation

1. Did delivery support content? Generally? Some of the time? Not often?
2. Was the Scripture read smoothly?
3. Did I communicate the ethos of the Scripture?
4. Did I communicate the ethos of the sermon?
5. Were the ethos of the Scripture reading and of the sermon at variance?

Review chapter five for information and exercises to help oral interpretation.

Bibliography

Books

Barth, Karl. *The Preaching of the Gospel.* Trans. by B. E. Hooke. Philadelphia: Westminster Press, 1963.

Barth, Karl. *The Word of God and the Word of Man.* Trans. by Douglas Horton. London: Hodder and Stoughton, 1928.

Bartow, Charles L. *The Preaching Moment: A Guide to Sermon Delivery.* Abingdon Preacher's Library Series, ed. by William D. Thompson. Nashville: Abingdon Press, 1980.

Benson, Dennis. *Electric Evangelism.* Nashville: Abingdon Press, 1973.

Benthall, Jonathan and Ted Polhemus, eds. *The Body as a Medium of Expression.* New York: E. P. Dutton and Co., 1975.

Broadus, John A. *A Treatise on the Preparation and Delivery of Sermons.* Revised by E. C. Dargan. New York: George H. Doran Co., 1898.

Brooks, Dieth, Eugene Bahn, and L. Lamont Okey. *The Communicative Act of Oral Interpretation.* Boston: Allyn and Bacon, Inc., 1975.

Brooks, Phillips. *Lectures on Preaching.* Grand Rapids: Baker Book House, 1978 reprint.

Brown, H. C., Jr. *A Quest for Reformation in Preaching.* Waco, Texas: Word Books, 1968.

Brown, H. C., Jr., H. Gordon Clinard, and Jesse J. Northcutt. *Steps to the Sermon.* Nashville: Broadman Press, 1963.

Caird, G. B. *The Language and Imagery of the Bible.* Philadelphia: Westminster Press, 1980.

Chartier, Myron R. *Preaching as Communication: An Interpersonal Perspective.* Abingdon Preacher's Library Series, ed. by William D. Thompson. Nashville: Abingdon Press, 1981.

Danielou, Jean. *Christ and Us.* Trans. by Walter Roberts. New York: Sheed and Ward, 1961.

Eisenson, Jon and Paul H. Boase. *Basic Speech.* 3rd ed. New York: Macmillan, 1975.

Eisenson, Jon. *Voice and Diction.* 3rd ed. New York: Macmillan, 1974.

Ellens, J. Harold. *Models of Religious Broadcasting.* Grand Rapids, Michigan: Eerdmans, 1974.

Grasso, Domenico. *Proclaiming God's Message: A Study in the Theology of Preaching.* South Bend, Indiana: The University of Notre Dame Press, 1965.

Harper, Nancy. *Human Communication Theory: The History of a Paradigm.* Rochelle Park, New Jersey: Hayden Books Co., Inc., 1979.

Hovland, Carl I., Irving L. Janis, and Harold H. Kelly. *Communication and Persuasion.* New Haven, Connecticut: Yale University Press, 1953.

Hughey, Jim D. and Arlis W. Johnson. *Speech Communication: Foundations and Challenges.* New York: Macmillan, 1975.

Jackson, B. F., Jr. *You and Communication in the Church.* Waco, Texas: Word Books, 1974.

Klepper, Joseph T. *The Effects of Mass Communication.* Glencoe, Illinois: Free Press, Inc., 1960.

Knapp, Mark L. *Nonverbal Communication in Human Interaction.* New York: Holt, Rinehart and Winston, 1972.

Lischer, Richard. *A Theology of Preaching: The Dynamics of the Gospel.* Abingdon Preacher's Library Series, ed. by William D. Thompson. Nashville: Abingdon Press, 1981.

Mehrabian, Albert. *Nonverbal Communication.* Chicago: Aldine-Atherton, 1972.

Oliver, Robert T. *History of Public Speaking in America.* Boston: Allyn and Bacon, Inc., 1965.

Ott, Heinrich. *Theology and Preaching*. Trans. by Harold Knight. Philadelphia: Westminster Press, 1961.

Read, David H. C. *The Communication of the Gospel*. London: SCM Press, Ltd., 1952.

Rossiter, Charles M., Jr. and W. Barnett Pearce. *Communicating Personally: A Theory of Interpersonal Communication and Human Relationships*. New York: Bobbs-Merrill Co., 1975.

Sangster, W. E. *The Approach to Preaching*. Philadelphia: Westminster Press, 1952.

Sarrett, Lew, William Trufant Foster, and Alma Johnson Sarrett. *Basic Principles of Speech*. 3rd ed. Boston: Houghton Mifflin Co., 1958.

Siegman, Aaron W. and Stanley Feldstein, eds. *Nonverbal Behavior and Communication*. Hillsdale, New Jersey: Lawrence Erlbaum Associates, 1978.

Spurgeon, Charles Haddon. *Lectures to My Students*. Grand Rapids: Zondervan Press, 1945.

Steimle, Edmund A., Morris J. Niedenthal, and Charles L. Rice. *Preaching the Story*. Philadelphia: Fortress Press, 1980.

Stevenson, Dwight E. and Charles F. Diehl. *Reaching People from the Pulpit*. New York: Harper and Row, 1958.

Webber, Robert E. *God Still Speaks: A Biblical View of Christian Communication*. Nashville: Nelson, 1980.

Articles

Bailey, Raymond, "Vital Preaching!," *The Baptist Program,* November, 1974.

Bluck, John, "Beyond Neutrality: A Christian Critique of the Media," *Risk Book Series,* No. 3, 1978.

Brooks, R. T., "Preaching in an Audio-Visual Age," *Baptist Quarterly,* Vol. 29, July, 1981.

Dunnam, Spurgeon M., Jr., "Guidelines for the Church for Ministry Through the Mass Media," *Perkins Journal of Theology,* Vol. 28, Summer, 1975.

Ellens, Harold J., "Psychodynamics in Mass Media Society," *Journal of Psychology and Theology,* Vol. 7, Fall, 1979.

Fore, William F., "Communication: A Complex Task for the Church," *Christian Century,* Vol. 92, July 9, 1975.

Hesselgrave, David J., "'Gold From Egypt': The Contribution of Rhetoric to Cross-cultural Communication," *Missiology,* Vol. 4, January, 1976.

Joregenson, Knud, "Models of Communication in the New Testament," *Missiology,* Vol. 4, October, 1976.

Kehl, D. G., "Have You Committed Verbicide Today?," *Christianity Today,* Vol. 22, January 27, 1978.

Meister, J. W. Gregg, "Mass Media Ministry: Understanding Television," *Theology Today,* Vol. 37, October, 1980.

Nichols, J. Randall, "Towards a Theological View of Responsibility in Communication," *The Princeton Seminary Bulletin,* Vol. 68, Winter, 1976.

Montgomery, John Warwick, "Mass Communication and Scriptural Proclamation," *The Evangelical Quarterly,* Vol. 49, January-March, 1977.

Muggeridge, Malcolm, "Christ and the Media," *Journal of the Evangelical Society,* Vol. 21, September, 1978.

Taylor, Roy, "So What?," *The Journal of Pastoral Practice,* Vol. 4, No. 4, 1980.

Towne, Edgar A., "Communicating a Message and Believing a Message," *Encounter,* Vol. 37, Winter, 1976.

Watson, Richard G., "What's Wrong with Preaching Today?," *Christianity Today,* October 25, 1974.